I0569303

A SECOND CHANCE

THOMAS E. SMITH

Copyright © 2026 Thomas E. Smith

All rights reserved.

No part of this publication may be reproduced, distributed, or transmitted in any form or by any means, including photocopying, recording, or other electronic or mechanical methods, without the prior written permission of the publisher, except in the case of brief quotations embodied in critical reviews and certain other non-commercial uses permitted by copyright law. For permission requests, email the publisher:

Attention: Permissions Coordinator

Welcome To The Storm Publishing!

info@w2tspublishing.org

Ordering Information:

Quantity sales. Special discounts are available on quantity purchases by corporations, associations, and others. For details, contact the publisher at the email address above.

Orders by U.S. trade bookstores and wholesalers.

Library of Congress Control Number: 2025926138

ISBN: 978-1-966612-96-4

Cover Design: Olaniyan Bukola

First Printed Edition: January 2026

Printed in the United States of America

DEDICATION

To Alberta Flentroy, Ann Radford (may she rest in peace), Bobby McMahan, Bobby Richardson, Cherly Whaley and Terry Riley—your unwavering support and belief in me have been the guiding lights in my journey. You were not just teachers; you were mentors who inspired me to reach for the stars.

You instilled in me the courage to persevere, reminding me that no matter how daunting the challenges may seem, I could overcome them. Your words of encouragement echoed in my heart, urging me to never give up and to keep moving forward in life. This book is a testament to your influence and the profound impact you have had on my life.

To you, dear reader, I dedicate this journey. Thank you for being a part of my story and for finding a piece of life within these chapters. Your presence makes this endeavor worthwhile, and I hope my words resonate with you as they have with me.

Table of Contents

ACKNOWLEDGMENTS..1

CHAPTER 1 2

Flashbacks..2

CHAPTER 2 16

Life Before the Incident..16

CHAPTER 3 36

The Turning Point..36

CHAPTER 4 49

The Night of the Incident...49

CHAPTER 5 60

The Road to Recovery..60

CHAPTER 6 66

Educational Journey...66

CHAPTER 7 79

Professional Life...79

CHAPTER 8 91

Parallel Experiences - Good and Bad.......................................91

About the Author...99

ACKNOWLEDGMENTS

I extend my deepest gratitude to God, the one who saved me from the storms that threatened to engulf my life. In my darkest moments, especially during my time in the hospital, I felt the power of prayer surrounding me, lifting me up when I was at my lowest. To all those who prayed for me, your faith and love were my anchors.

To all those who pick up this book, thank you for granting me the opportunity to share my journey. Your willingness to receive my words has given me a chance to live again, and for that, I am eternally grateful.

CHAPTER 1

Flashbacks

"The wound is the place where the Light enters you."
– Rumi

So, here's what I want you to do, with God helping you. Take your everyday life — your sleeping, eating, working, and moving through the world — and place it before God as an offering. Embrace what God does for you because it's the strongest response you can give him. Don't let yourself become so adjusted to your culture that you move through it without thought. Fix your attention on God instead. When you do, the change starts from the inside. You begin to see what he asks of you, and you can respond without delay. The culture around you pulls you toward its own level of immaturity, but God pulls you upward. He brings out your best and shapes you into maturity.

But sometimes this transformation begins in a place marked by deep pain. The word "wounded" carries a weight that goes beyond physical injury. It points to the emotional and spiritual suffering we all face. Wounds, whether visible or hidden, can leave us feeling exposed and broken. They can strike without warning and shake the foundations of our lives.

Yet even in this brokenness, God is present. Isaiah 53:5 reminds us, "But it was our sins that did that to him, that ripped and tore and crushed him, our sins. He took the punishment, and that made us whole. Through his bruises we get healed." This healing, this wholeness, is what God offers in exchange for our wounds. When we bring our pain to him — our daily struggles, doubts, and hurts — he uses it to reshape us from the inside out and lead us into deeper maturity and a steadier walk with him.

Isaiah 53:5 But it was our sins that did that to him, that ripped and tore and crushed him—our sins! He took the punishment, and that made us whole. Through his bruises, we get healed.

To me, being wounded is more than a physical injury; it is an assault on the core of who we are, a disruption of our sense of security and well-being. It breaks our assumptions about safety and invulnerability and forces us to face how fragile life can be. This wound can take many forms, whether through betrayal, loss, or trauma. Like a knife cutting through flesh, the words and actions that wound us leave scars that run deep and change the way our hearts and minds work. These scars may not be visible, but they shape our perceptions and decisions and influence how we move through the world.

What makes being wounded so damaging is how it grows inside us. Unhealed emotions sit beneath the surface and build into resentment, anger, and bitterness. These feelings create an internal environment that clouds our judgment and distorts how we see the world. Over time this mix can begin to take over from the inside and trap us in a cycle of despair and hopelessness. Breaking free from that cycle takes real courage and honest self-reflection, because it forces us to face the wounds we try to hide.

But the road ahead was not without challenges. As the days moved closer to prom night, the pressure grew and the expectations settled on my shoulders like weight I wasn't ready for. Doubt sat in the back of my mind and pushed against my confidence, threatening to break my resolve. Even with that uncertainty, I found support in the people around me — the shared laughter, the quiet conversations, and the familiar bonds that helped us face the strain of adolescence. Together we managed the chaos, steadying each other through the highs and lows of teenage life and coming out stronger for it.

There was something unspoken in the way we held on to one another, as if we all sensed that this night could mark a shift. Prom wasn't about the lights or the music; it was a chance to claim a moment of joy after everything we had faced. For me, it felt like a test. Could I show up, keep my head up, and let the night remind me that I was still here? I didn't have the answer yet, but I knew I had to try.

As the day of the prom approached, I made a quiet promise to myself to accept the uncertainty, confront my fears head on, and move with confidence even when everything felt unstable. I knew that whatever came next, I had enough strength to face it, overcome what stood in my way, and rise above it. So, when I stood inside the Youth Center, surrounded by flashing lights and loud music, I repeated that promise. I told myself to accept whatever the future brought, take every opportunity that came my way, and hold on to the lessons from that Friday night. Because in the middle of the noise and excitement, I realized how much power a single moment can carry.

Each beat of the music felt like a heartbeat, a reminder that I had survived. Every smiling face around me reflected resilience. The night stretched ahead like a blank page waiting to be written. I promised myself I would not hold back. No more hiding behind fear—this night, I would live.

On that Friday April 13, 1990, I stepped into the Youth Center. The familiar scents of sweat and excitement mingled with the rhythm of the music, filling the space with energy. Laughter and joy pulsed through the crowd, a reflection of young people seeking connection. As I moved through the center, my father's nickname for me, "Nugget," echoed in my mind. It was more than a name; it was a badge of honor and a reminder of the bond between father and son. In that moment, a surge of warmth and nostalgia filled me, as if he were dancing beside me, urging me to cherish the present while honoring the past.

Nights like these, with music blaring and excitement in the air, gave me a confidence built from countless hours perfecting my dance moves and charm. For me, the Youth Center was more than a place to socialize. It was a sanctuary where I could escape life's pressures, a space to breathe freely amid flashing lights and pulsing beats. As I moved through the crowded halls, anticipation grew with each step. Exhilaration coursed through me. The camaraderie of friends and the pull of the dance floor combined to make me feel invincible, as if anything could happen on a night like this. I stepped onto the floor, and the girls' eyes followed me, their smiles pulling me into a whirl of movement and laughter. Dancing there, the cares of the world faded, replaced by a sense of freedom I could find only in that moment.

This space had become my stage, and for a few hours, I could forget the expectations, the disappointments, and the silence waiting outside. Every beat reminded me that I was alive, that I mattered, that here—right here—I was seen. The sweat on my brow, the ache in my muscles, even the pull of my lungs for air—it all added to the electricity that made these nights feel alive. I fed off the energy of those around me; their joy became my fuel. We weren't just dancing; we were escaping together.

The Youth Center, usually a hub of activity, seemed to thrum with even greater energy that evening. The air carried the promise of adventure, and the music pulsed through me like a second heartbeat, matching the rhythm of my excitement. It was a night full of possibility, brimming with the potential for unforgettable moments and lasting memories.

Each song seemed to carry a hidden message, as if speaking directly to my soul. There was a strange beauty in how the chaos outside these walls could not reach me here. Time blurred. Faces became streaks of color and light. For a while, it felt as if the world had paused, letting us be young and limitless. I had no idea how precious that feeling was or how soon it would be taken from me.

Little did I know then, as I reveled in the warmth of friendship and the promise of the night, that fate had other plans. The events of that evening would unravel my sense of security in ways I could never have imagined, casting me into a sea of uncertainty and challenge.

In hindsight, the signs were there—subtle, quiet, almost easy to miss. A glance that lasted too long. A hush that fell over a group too suddenly. I did not notice it then, lost in the rhythm and the lights, but the night had already begun to shift. The energy, once electric, started to hum with something darker. I brushed it off. We all did. We did not want to believe that joy could turn on us so quickly. But joy, like anything else, is fragile.

Beneath the laughter, a nagging unease remained—a feeling that some dark secret hid in the shadows. The tension in the air was subtle but persistent, like a whisper I could not quite hear. I pushed the fear aside, choosing to trust the music, the friendship, and the fleeting moments of happiness.

Because that is what we do when we are young—we believe we are untouchable. We think fear is just a shadow, easily ignored if we dance hard enough, laugh loud enough, or stay close enough to the light. But darkness waits. On nights like these, it waits quietly, patiently, just beyond the edge of the spotlight.

Even as whispers of doubt crept into my mind, threatening to engulf me in a maelstrom of insecurity and self-doubt, I refused to succumb. I held on to the thrill of victory—the memory of triumph on the track field, the taste of success still sweet on our lips—as a beacon of hope in the face of adversity.

I could still feel the sun on my skin, the grit of the track beneath my shoes, and the unified rhythm of my teammates' footsteps beside me. That race had tested more than our speed—it had tested our willpower, our unity, our belief in one another. We had run not just to win, but to prove something— to ourselves, to those who doubted us, and to the past that tried to hold us back. In that proof, I found power. It reminded me that I had what it took to rise, endure, and win again.

On that hallowed ground, in the middle of the crowd's roar and the pounding of our hearts, we had achieved the seemingly impossible. We had defied the odds and emerged victorious, our spirits lifted by triumph and vindication. As I stood atop the podium, the cheers ringing in my ears, I knew that no taunt or jeer could diminish the pride and accomplishment swelling inside me.

I closed my eyes for a moment, letting the sound wash over me like a wave, grounding myself in the reality of what we had just done. It felt like a message from the universe—proof that pain and struggle could give birth to something meaningful.

For the first time in a long while, I felt seen, not just by others, but by myself. That win was not just about speed or medals; it was about reclaiming a part of me I thought I had lost. There was clarity in that moment, a quiet realization that strength is not always loud—it is in the stillness after the storm.

Little did I know, as I lost myself in laughter and dance, that my life would change forever that night—shredding the sense of normalcy and setting me on a path I could never have imagined. That night drew an invisible line across my timeline: before and after.

As the night wore on and the music reached a fever pitch, it happened—a moment that shattered the fragile veneer of normalcy and plunged me into a nightmare I would struggle to escape. A gunshot cut through the air like a jagged blade, sending shockwaves of terror through the crowd. Laughter twisted into screams. The vibrant night erupted into chaos.

One second I was surrounded by rhythm and light; the next, panic swallowed everything. The sound echoed off the walls, bouncing between disbelief and fear. People scattered like leaves in a storm, moving without direction, eyes wide with confusion. Some dropped to the floor, others ran, but all of us shared the same realization: everything had changed. The safety we felt was gone, ripped away in a heartbeat. That single shot became the dividing line—before and after, innocence and experience.

Time slowed, stretched thin and surreal. My body surged forward instinctively, adrenaline pumping, senses sharpened by pure survival. Every sound grew louder, every shadow more menacing. My heart thundered in my ears as sweat dripped unchecked. The air felt thick, almost suffocating, as I struggled to maintain balance amid the spiraling confusion.

I heard a name shouted—perhaps a friend's, perhaps my own—but the voice was swallowed by the chaos. I stumbled over a fallen chair, hands trembling, legs weak. My mind screamed for clarity, but thoughts came like static. Was I hit? Were they okay? Where was the exit? Faces blurred, voices collided, yet somehow I kept moving. My only instinct was to survive, to make it out alive. There was no room for fear, only motion.

Looking back now, through the haze of memory, I marvel at the twists and turns that brought me to this point. What began as a night of innocent revelry and youthful abandon had become a crucible of pain and suffering—a trial by fire that tested the limits of my strength in ways I could never have imagined.

That night etched itself into me, not just as a memory but as a mark on my soul. I carry the echo of that gunshot, the faces of those who did not make it out, the weight of what we lost. I also carry something else—the knowledge that I survived, that I had to make the living matter. Trauma does not leave clean wounds. It festers, it persists. But it also demands reckoning. Slowly, I began to answer that call.

Amid the chaos and uncertainty, there was a hope—a spark of steadfastness that refused to be extinguished. Even in the darkest moments, there exists the potential for redemption and renewal, the chance to rise from the ashes and forge a new path forward.

Somewhere inside me, something chose not to give up. Not that night. Not after. I sought cover instinctively, finding refuge in the shadows even as fear wrapped tightly around me. In those moments, I realized there was no escaping what had just occurred. That gunshot echoed not just in the room but through the core of my being, leaving devastation in its wake.

It pierced more than the silence—it fractured something inside me. I clutched my knees to my chest, trying to disappear into the corner, as if stillness could make me invisible. My breathing was ragged, each inhalation a reminder that I was still here, still alive. But the guilt of surviving began to creep in almost immediately. I wanted to cry, to scream, but my throat was frozen. My eyes scanned the darkness, searching for something familiar, something safe—but everything had changed.

Emerging cautiously from my hiding, I faced a scene of utter destruction—bodies strewn like rag dolls, faces contorted with pain and terror, anguished cries echoing like a mournful song. Disoriented, I felt adrift on a sea of uncertainty, tossed by fate's cruel winds with no compass to guide me. The fragile nature of life lay bare before me, raw and humbling.

The dance floor that once held joy now reeked of tragedy. Shoes without owners, shattered phones, torn shirts—a thousand small stories left behind in the wreckage. I stepped carefully, each footfall a prayer. My legs trembled beneath me, but I kept moving. I wasn't sure what I was looking for—maybe a friend, maybe clarity, maybe a reason this happened—but I had to look. Grief hung in the air like smoke, choking and thick. This was the kind of night that carved permanent scars.

Yet even there, in the heart of despair, a sliver of hope flickered—a small, stubborn light promising redemption and renewal. Amid the wreckage that had shattered so much, I made a silent vow: to rise from the ashes, defy the cards dealt to me, and emerge stronger, braver, and more determined than ever.

Because hope wasn't just a feeling—it was survival. In the darkest moments, it was the only thing that could anchor me. I didn't know how or when I would heal, but I knew I had to. I owed it to myself. I owed it to those who didn't walk out. From that night forward, I carried their names like stones in my pocket—heavy but grounding.

Instinct and adrenaline fueled my flight. Pain tore through every fiber, yet there was no time to falter. The world blurred—a storm of colors, sounds, and panic threatening to drown my senses. I stumbled suddenly, falling hard; agony blazed like wildfire, threatening to snuff out the fragile spark still burning inside me. But I refused to give in. Clinging to hope's flicker, I fought back from the brink, breathing and struggling with every ounce of strength.

My knees hit the floor with a brutal thud, but I pushed myself up, teeth clenched, fists shaking. My vision pulsed with tears and dizziness, yet I fixed my eyes on the hallway ahead. It was blurry and distant, but still there. Someone grabbed my arm. I couldn't tell if they were trying to help or stop me, but I pulled away on instinct. This was survival stripped of reason or grace. Each breath felt like a fight. Each step felt earned. Somewhere in me, I knew this moment marked a divide between who I had been and who I was becoming.

Days and nights blended together as I drifted between life and death, caught in pain and uncertainty. Yet that flicker of hope stayed bright and fierce, a small light pulling me through the darkest moments. It felt fragile and easy to break, but it was the only thing I could hold as everything else collapsed around me.

Some nights I drifted into a quiet space, not fully asleep and not fully awake. In those moments, I imagined light coming through a window, imagined laughter, imagined a hand that was not covered in latex. I held on to those small visions. They felt distant, but they reminded me that something beyond the pain still existed.

The hospital walls closed around me, sterile and unyielding, with the steady beep of machines reminding me how fragile life could be. Death sat close, but giving up never felt like an option. I chose to fight, to pull my future out of uncertainty and shape something new.

The nurses became familiar faces, their voices soft yet urgent. I learned to read the glances between them. Some carried worry, others hope. I counted ceiling tiles more times than I could remember, whispered prayers into the dark when sleep refused to come. Pain came in waves, but so did strength. I did not know its source, only that it existed. That alone was enough to keep moving.

In adversity's depths, I discovered an unknown strength, an adaptability born of necessity, a flame of hope unextinguished by fate's harsh winds. Each day brought new battles—setbacks and doubts that tested my resolve. But step by step, I reclaimed life's gift, loosening despair's hold as a phoenix rises from ashes.

Progress was slow. A small movement in my fingers felt like triumph. A sip of water, a whispered word, a moment without pain—each became a milestone. Every win reminded me that I was still here, still fighting. Some days were harder than others. I no longer measured progress by speed. I measured it by will. And that will was growing.

Bound to a hospital bed, tubes serving as lifelines, I pledged to embrace this second chance with courage and tenacity. To live each moment as if it were my last. Life, I learned, is a precious, fleeting gift—a brief spark of wonder in a chaotic world. The road ahead was long and daunting, but I faced it with unwavering hope and strength born from suffering.

The thought of leaving that room began to feel real. I

pictured myself walking again, hearing laughter beyond the sterile halls, tasting food not served on a plastic tray. That vision pulled me forward. I did not just want to live; I wanted to feel alive. Slowly, my body began to remember how.

Closing my eyes each night, I found peace in knowing that, no matter what, I would meet the future with courage. In adversity's depths, I discovered the true measure of my strength—a fierce, unextinguishable flame of hope.

Peace did not mean the absence of fear. It meant choosing to stand in the middle of it and still believe. I understood now that healing was not just physical. Parts of me were bruised and bent far beyond what any doctor could treat. But I was willing to face those too. Not all at once—just a little at a time.

From that crucible arose a revelation: the life-altering power of second chances. This gift shaped my path and inspired a journey of self-discovery, faith, and renewed purpose. Each step forward carried a mix of doubt and determination, but with resolve, I seized life anew.

There were days when I did not know what came next. But that no longer scared me as it once had. I had faced death and survived. I had lost things I could never get back. But I had also gained something no one could take away. I had purpose. I had direction. And I was not done yet.

The echoes of that night never faded—a reminder of life's fragile beauty and the preciousness of every breath. Yet within the darkness, I found light: a beacon of hope shining through despair, guiding me onward.

Even now, when the world quiets, I still hear the echoes. They no longer haunt me. They remind me of how far I have come, of how far I still have to go, and of how every step forward is a quiet act of defiance against the darkness that once tried to take me.

Drawn to stories of those who overcame, I found strength and inspiration—proof that the human spirit endures and triumphs. Armed with newfound steadfastness, I ventured forth to reclaim my life, shedding old chains and embracing possibilities.

I began to dream again, not just of survival but of building something more. Perhaps it was time to tell my story. Perhaps someone else needed to hear that they, too, could make it through. The idea scared me, but it also stirred something alive inside me.

Stepping beyond the hospital walls, exhilaration surged— freedom reborn, a life reclaimed with passion and purpose. Yet the past's echoes lingered, a solemn reminder of both fragility and strength. With gratitude and humility, I faced the future, each step a triumph, each breath a gift on the journey toward lasting redemption and renewal.

The sun felt different that day. Brighter. Warmer. Yet unfamiliar, as if I were meeting it for the first time. I didn't know what would come next. All I knew was that change was near. Somewhere beyond that first step lay a new beginning, one I hadn't planned for but was ready to meet.

This Where It All Began

CHAPTER 2

Life Before the Incident

"Dreams are a dream or an imagination. To me, my dream
was the opposite in my life."

-Isaiah 43:18-19

"Remember ye not the former things, nor consider the things of old. Be alert, be present. I'm about to do something brand new. It's bursting out! Don't you see it? There it is! I'm making a road through the desert, rivers in the badlands."

Friday nights were always infused with a sense of possibility, the promise of something extraordinary lingering in the air like an unspoken invitation to adventure. The sun began its slow descent, casting long shadows and painting the sky in hues of pink and orange, while the world seemed to hold its breath in anticipation. But for me, Friday the 13th, 1990, would prove to be more than just another night of youthful exuberance. It became a turning point, a fork in the road that altered the trajectory of my existence in ways I could never have foreseen.

The vibrant hum of the neighborhood grew louder, filled with the laughter of friends, the faint strains of music drifting from distant houses, and the undeniable energy that coursed through our community. In the air was a tension—a mix of excitement and unease—as if the universe were conspiring to deliver a moment that would forever change my reality. I felt it in the way my heart raced, in tune with the symphony of possibilities awaiting me. Each Friday night was a canvas on which we painted our dreams, yet this one felt different, charged with an electricity hinting at the start of a new chapter in my life.

Reflecting on the days leading up to that fateful night, memories flicker like fragments of a dream, each a snapshot of a life that existed before the incident—a life filled with hope, ambition, and an unwavering belief in the power of possibility. The week had been marked by a blend of excitement and anxiety, a cocktail of emotions stirring within me as I navigated the routines of teenage life. Each morning, I awoke with a sense of purpose, my mind racing with thoughts of the future and what lay beyond graduation.

There was a restlessness in my soul that week, as if something deep inside knew life was about to shift. I found myself lingering longer in conversations, taking mental snapshots of smiles and laughter I feared might soon become memories. Even mundane tasks—walking to class, flipping through textbooks, waiting for the final bell—took on a strange significance. I began to notice the smallest details: sunlight filtering through classroom blinds, sneakers squeaking on polished floors, the scent of pencil shavings and cafeteria food. It all felt like a buildup, a quiet crescendo leading to an unknown but inevitable climax.

The familiar hallways of Crossett High School echoed with the chatter of my peers, each conversation a reminder of the collective dreams we shared, even as I grappled with the reality that our paths might soon diverge. In these fleeting moments—sitting in class, exchanging knowing glances with friends, daydreaming about what lay beyond the horizon—I felt the weight of my aspirations pressing down on me. There was an urgency in my spirit, a desire to grasp the fleeting nature of youth and mold it into something tangible. As I navigated the complexities of friendships and the bittersweetness of impending change, I couldn't shake the feeling that each decision brought me closer to that pivotal moment—an intersection of fate and choice I could sense but had not yet seen.

From as far back as I can remember, I harbored dreams that burned brightly within me, igniting a steadfast purpose that guided me through the trials of adolescence. They gave me something to hold on to when the world felt uncertain and unfamiliar. I would lie in bed at night, staring at the ceiling, my mind racing with visions of a future where I had conquered my fears and achieved greatness. In those quiet hours, I felt closest to who I truly was. The dreams I nurtured were not idle fantasies; they were the lifeblood that sustained me during moments of doubt. They reminded me that I was meant for more, even when no one else said it aloud. Like many children, I had aspirations that bordered on the unbelievable—a longing for something greater, beyond the confines of my surroundings. I refused to let my environment define the limits of my imagination. My dreams took shape in vivid colors, splashed across my mind like a canvas waiting to be painted. I envisioned myself on grand stages, performing feats that defied expectation, basking in the applause of those who believed in my potential.

Each aspiration was a promise to myself, a vow that I would not succumb to the limitations imposed by circumstance. That vow became a silent mantra I carried daily. During those formative years, I discovered the exhilaration of pursuing a passion, dedicating myself wholeheartedly to a vision that seemed distant yet tantalizingly close. With every step, I inched closer to that imagined future. With every beat of my heart, I stoked the flames of my ambition, determined to transform the whispers of my dreams into a resounding declaration of self-worth.

Martin Luther King Jr. once spoke of a dream—a vision of equality and justice that transcended the boundaries of race and prejudice. His words resonated deeply, stirring a recognition of the renewing power of dreams—the ability to envision a future beyond the limitations of the present. I remember hearing his speech for the first time in school, my eyes fixed on the grainy video as his voice echoed through the classroom. In that moment, something shifted. King's dream was not merely a personal aspiration; it was a call to action, a reminder that dreams can unite us, inspire change, and forge paths toward a brighter future.

I often reflected on the significance of his message, realizing that my dreams, while rooted in personal ambition, echoed a universal longing for fulfillment and purpose. It helped me see that my hopes were not just about success— they were about making a difference. King's dream became a guiding thread in my aspirations, reminding me that pursuing dreams is not solely an individual journey but a collective endeavor with the power to uplift communities. It challenged me to think beyond myself and ask how my goals could benefit others. I understood that dreams could serve as beacons of hope in the darkest times, lighting the way forward even when the path seemed obscured by doubt and fear. Each time I faced adversity, I recalled King's words, allowing them to fortify my resolve and remind me that the struggle for dreams is a noble pursuit—a sentiment that stayed with me as I approached that fateful night in 1990. Even then, I knew I was moving toward something greater than myself.

As a child, I would sit with my friends, watching cars pass by, each one a symbol of possibility. We would point and proclaim, "That's my car, that's my car," our voices brimming with the innocent certainty of youth. In those moments, the world felt boundless, full of opportunities waiting to be seized. We didn't know exactly what the future held, but we believed it would be something big—something better. I can vividly recall the laughter that erupted from our group, the carefree banter that captured the spirit of our youth, as we made grand declarations about our futures, each of us imagining a life filled with promise. The street became our stage, our imaginations painting vivid scenes of who we might become. The cars that sped by were more than vehicles; they embodied the dreams we held close, the aspirations that teased us with the allure of the unknown.

They were tangible reminders of the freedom we yearned for—the freedom to escape our circumstances, to break free from the confines of our small-town lives and venture into a world full of opportunity. Those childhood afternoons became our sanctuary, a time when we allowed ourselves to dream without fear or limits. In those moments of playful imagining, I felt a deep sense of camaraderie with my friends, a shared belief that we were destined for greatness and that no dream was too lofty to achieve. We didn't speak of hardships at home or the struggles that awaited us—only of the bright futures we hoped to build. As we laughed and shared our dreams, I couldn't help but wonder how far each of us would go, how our lives might intersect, and whether the choices we made would guide us toward the futures we envisioned. That feeling of togetherness, of daring to hope, lingered long after the sun dipped below the horizon.

For me, basketball was more than just a game—it was a

lifeline, a way to escape the challenges of my childhood. It offered structure where there was chaos and focus where there was uncertainty. The familiar squeak of sneakers on the polished gym floor, the rhythmic thump of the ball, and the collective breath of anticipation from onlookers created an atmosphere that felt almost magical. It was the one place where I felt fully alive, completely in control.

I still vividly recall the makeshift basketball goal my brother and I fashioned from a wooden box and an old bicycle rim, a mark of our resourcefulness and determination. That rickety hoop became the center of our world, a space where dreams took flight and the weight of daily life faded away. We spent hours shooting hoops, the sun beating down as we laughed and encouraged one another, forging a bond through our shared love of the game. Even in the heat and dust, those were moments of pure joy, of dreaming without limits. Each basket was a small victory, a step toward something greater.

Basketball was where I found solace, where the noise of the outside world dissolved into a blur, and I could lose myself in the rhythm of dribbling and the thrill of shooting. Each game became a dance, a choreography of movement that let me express myself, channel my frustrations, and dream of the day I would step onto a grander stage—the courts of the NBA. It was in those moments of play that I discovered my identity, the essence of who I was and who I aspired to become.

From the moment I first picked up a basketball, I was hooked. There was something intoxicating about the rhythm of the game—the thud of the ball against the pavement, the rush of adrenaline as I sprinted down the court, eyes fixed on the hoop. The joy of sinking a perfect shot sent waves of euphoria through my veins, fueling my drive to improve and pushing me to test my limits with each passing day.

My passion for the game became an all-consuming fire, burning brightly within me and guiding my path forward. I could recall the hours spent practicing alone, imagining the cheers of the crowd as I executed flawless crossovers and perfect layups, the world fading until it was just me and the game. I was driven not only by the desire to succeed but also by the belief that basketball held the key to a future beyond my wildest dreams. In my mind, I pictured myself wearing the jersey of my favorite NBA team, my name on the back as I stepped onto the court, the crowd erupting in applause, their energy fueling my performance. This vision became a guiding star, a relentless motivator that propelled me through adolescence, ensuring every setback was met with resolve—to keep pushing, keep dreaming, and keep working toward the future I so desperately craved.

As a child, my dreams were simple yet profound—to become an NBA player, to escape the confines of my rough neighborhood, to create a future filled with promise and opportunity. I envisioned myself not only as a player but as a symbol of hope for others facing similar struggles, proof that dreams could transcend circumstances. I dedicated myself wholeheartedly to that pursuit, spending countless hours on the playground, honing my skills, and refining my craft.

The basketball court became my sanctuary, a space where I could channel my energy and emotions into something tangible. I immersed myself in the sport, studying the moves of my idols, practicing tirelessly to perfect my jump shot, dribbling, and footwork. I watched every game I could, analyzing players' techniques, dissecting strategies, and applying the lessons to my own practice. With each dribble, I carved a path toward the future I envisioned, determined to make my mark. Commitment to my dream became a daily ritual, a promise to myself to do whatever it took to succeed, even in the face of obstacles that threatened to derail my ambitions. In those early years, I learned the value of resilience and perseverance—lessons that would guide me through challenges yet to come.

Visualization became my most potent tool in pursuing my dreams, allowing me to transcend the limits of my reality and envision a future filled with opportunity. I would study the basketball, committing every detail to memory, then close my eyes and recreate it in my mind with vivid clarity. In those moments of focused imagination, I transported myself to a world where I was unstoppable, where the air buzzed with the excitement of competition and the thrill of victory. I could hear the crowd's cheers, feel the weight of the jersey on my shoulders, and sense the energy that surrounded me as I stepped onto the court. With every breath, I brought my dreams to life, letting the adrenaline fuel my determination to turn those visions into reality.

The more I practiced this mental rehearsal, the more vivid the imagery became, turning my aspirations into tangible experiences I could draw upon during games. I learned to harness the power of my mind, recognizing that the journey toward achieving my dreams depended as much on mental fortitude as on physical skill. In those moments of visualization, I became the architect of my destiny, crafting a future that shimmered with the promise of greatness. The world outside may have been filled with doubt and uncertainty, but in my mind, I was already living my dream, each moment a proof of the possibilities that awaited me.

As adolescence gave way to adulthood, the harsh realities of life began to intrude on my dreams, casting shadows over the once unshakable belief in my potential. Expectations, responsibilities, and the creeping weight of self-doubt threatened to unravel the intricate vision I had built from my aspirations. The laughter of my childhood friends, once a source of inspiration, now reminded me of the fleeting nature of youth and the inevitability of change. Each day brought new challenges, the kind that could easily snuff out the flickering flame of hope I had nurtured for so long. The path to success was not as straightforward as I had imagined; it was filled with obstacles that tested my resolve and forced me to confront the uncomfortable truth that not all dreams come true.

Whispers of doubt grew louder, accompanied by the advice of well-meaning voices urging me to be realistic, to temper my aspirations in a world that often rewarded conformity over ambition. Some offered guidance with kindness, others with a quiet skepticism that cut deeper than words. I found myself at a crossroads, weighing these conflicting messages against the realization that the dreams I once held dear now felt distant and unattainable. What had once seemed certain was beginning to slip through my fingers. Quiet moments became heavy with questions I did not yet know how to answer.

Despite my best efforts, the NBA dream remained elusive, a shimmering mirage on the horizon that seemed to retreat with each passing day. I chased it with everything I had, but the closer I got, the more impossible it felt. Late-night practices and early mornings of drills that once filled me with joy began to feel like burdens—an exhausting cycle that left me questioning the foundation of my dreams. I wondered if I was holding on too tightly to something never meant to be mine.

Friends who once shared my aspirations started to drift away, their paths diverging as they pursued different futures, and I felt a growing sense of isolation—a recognition that my dreams might not align with the reality around me. They moved on, and I stayed behind, clinging to a vision that felt like a ghost. The court, once a sacred space where I felt invincible, now felt like a battleground. Each missed shot and failed attempt reminded me that dreams require more than passion; they demand relentless dedication and a resilience I struggled to maintain.

As the weight of expectation settled on my shoulders, I grappled with the fear of failure—the nagging thought that my dreams were too lofty, that I was chasing shadows in a world where success seemed reserved for the fortunate few. The fear crept into my thoughts during quiet hours, making me question everything. Like many teenagers facing the harsh realities of adulthood, I found myself at a crossroads, realizing that not all dreams are meant to come true and wondering whether my unwavering faith in the impossible would only lead to heartbreak. The silence after missed opportunities became louder than any cheer I had ever heard.

Standing at the threshold of adulthood, I am acutely aware of the weight of responsibility on my shoulders. There is no turning back—only forward. The carefree days of childhood are gone, replaced by the sobering realization that the choices I make now will shape my future. Each decision feels monumental, a fork in the road that could lead to uncharted territory or deeper into the labyrinth of self-doubt. Sometimes I wish I could pause time and catch my breath. Friends and family watch with expectations, their hopes intertwined with my own as I navigate this turbulent phase of life. Yet, amid the chaos, I feel a flicker of resilience igniting—a stubborn refusal to abandon the dreams that have sustained me through my darkest days. Even when the path is unclear, I know I must keep moving forward.

Though the road ahead may be filled with challenges and uncertainty, I remain steadfast in my belief that every setback is a steppingstone on the path to greatness. I hold onto the memories of dreams that once burned brightly within me, letting them serve as a compass guiding me toward a future where anything is possible. The thought of giving up feels foreign, as if it would betray the very essence of who I am. Each challenge, every moment of doubt, becomes an opportunity for growth—a chance to prove not only to myself but to the world that dreams, no matter how elusive, are worth pursuing.

As I bid farewell to the innocence of youth and step into the journey ahead, I do so with a heart filled with hope. Hope for the dreams that still linger on the edges of my consciousness, waiting for the right moment to be realized. Hope for adventures yet to unfold and paths yet to be explored. In the crucible of adversity, I have learned that it is not the destination that defines us but the journey—the relentless pursuit of our dreams in the face of impossible odds. The memories of laughter, camaraderie, and unwavering belief from my youth remain etched in my heart, a reminder of the beauty of aspiration and the importance of holding onto hope. I understand now that the dreams of my childhood, while shaped by time, are still valid and worthy of pursuit.

They may take different forms, evolve, and adapt as I navigate the complexities of life, but they remain an integral part of who I am. As I step into the unknown, I carry with me the lessons learned through perseverance, the strength forged in the fires of challenge, and an unshakeable faith that the dreams of yesterday can still guide the path ahead.

Reflecting on the events that led to that fateful night in 1990, I am struck by the realization that life is a maze shaped by our dreams and aspirations. Each twist and turn, each moment of joy or despair, becomes a building block in the story of our existence. The decisions we make ripple through time, affecting not only our own lives but also the lives of those around us. I can see now how every choice I faced leading up to that pivotal night contributed to the formation of my destiny.

The late nights spent practicing on the basketball court, the friendships forged through shared dreams, and the moments of laughter and joy—all of these shaped the path that ultimately led me to that fateful evening. Though the road ahead remains full of challenges and setbacks, it is our belief in the power of our dreams that sustains us through the darkest days. This belief allows us to rise from disappointment and pursue our aspirations with renewed determination. Life is not merely a series of events but a collection of moments that define who we are and who we strive to become. As I navigate the complexities of existence, I carry with me the lessons learned and the dreams cherished, ready to embrace the adventures that lie ahead.

In the chapters that follow, I will explore the events that shaped my journey—the triumphs and setbacks, the moments of despair, and the hope that fueled my ambitions. Each experience, each obstacle, serves as a steppingstone toward self-discovery and resilience. I will recount the times I stumbled, the moments when the weight of the world pressed down upon me, and the instances when I found solace in hope and determination.

Though the road ahead may be uncertain, I remain steadfast in my belief that every setback is a prelude to greater achievement. Life is not linear; it is a winding path filled with unexpected twists, lessons learned in moments of darkness, and the guiding light of dreams that carry us through the shadows. As I share the stories that have shaped my existence, I do so with an open heart and an eager spirit, ready to face whatever challenges and triumphs lie ahead. With each word, I honor the dreams that have sustained me and acknowledge the resilience that has propelled me forward, aiming to inspire others navigating their own journeys of aspiration and discovery.

As the final weeks of high school approached, a mix of anticipation and unease settled over everything. The days felt longer, yet time seemed to move faster than ever. For many of my classmates, graduation signaled the end of one stage and the start of another—the first step into the unknown of adulthood. Some planned to move to distant states to chase their ambitions, while others chose to stay close to the familiarity of home. Prom plans, college acceptance news, and ideas for summer filled the conversations in the hallways.

Friends talked about their futures with voices that carried both excitement and fear as they tried to picture what was coming. I listened, hoping to absorb their confidence while keeping my own uncertainty to myself. For me, the transition felt both energizing and intimidating. I knew I was standing at a crossroads with possibilities ahead, yet everything still felt uncertain.

Each conversation reminded me of the choices I would soon have to make, the paths that could shape my future, and the goals waiting just beyond reach. I felt the weight of expectations on my shoulders, the pull for validation mixing with a quiet fear of the unknown. There was an unspoken pressure to appear certain, even though most of us were unsure.

As the days slipped away, I found myself moving between excitement and uncertainty. Summer waited with its promise of long, easy hours and simple distraction. Yet even in the middle of the laughter, a steady sense of responsibility pushed at the back of my mind, reminding me of the decisions ahead. I often looked out the window and watched the sun sink below the horizon, stretching shadows across the familiar landscape of my childhood.

In those quiet moments, I thought about the future—the

choices ahead, the opportunities I might meet, and the goals I still wanted to reach. My heart sped up at the idea of new experiences, but I also felt a sharp pull of nostalgia, a mix of longing for the simplicity of youth and the connections that shaped my early years. The faces of friends moved through my mind, each one tied to a memory, each laugh marking a moment I knew would stay with me.

The casual talk of classmates filled the air as we spent our last days of freedom, carried by the energy of being young. We celebrated what we had achieved, shared our plans for summer, and laughed in a way that echoed through the halls. Yet under all the excitement was a quiet sense of unease—the awareness that our easy days were ending and that adulthood, with all its demands, was close.

As the final bell rang and another school year ended, I felt a clear sense of finality settle in. The thought of leaving behind familiar routines, long-standing friendships, and the comfort of my hometown filled me with a mix of anticipation and unease. I realized these last moments of high school were the closing marks of my childhood, and I was intent on noticing each one.

For me, the move into adulthood came with a sobering truth—the dreams I held as a child were no longer enough to carry me into the demands of real life. The advice of well-meaning elders echoed in my mind, urging me to think beyond short-term pleasures and approach the future with intention and discipline. I often replayed conversations with my parents, their words steady with love and concern.

They had always encouraged me to pursue my passions, but now I could hear the worry beneath their words. It felt as if they were trying to guide me toward safer choices, urging me to prioritize practicality over dreams that once felt within reach. The distance between what I wanted and what they hoped for grew heavier, creating an internal pull that left me unsure of myself. I wanted to make them proud, yet I also felt the familiar spark of the dreams that had driven me since childhood.

As the first day of school approached, I was caught in the usual rush of preparations—new clothes, clean notebooks, and the sense of order that came with returning to a routine. The rhythm of school offered structure during the uncertainty of adolescence. Still, with every small task and passing moment, I felt a wave of nostalgia settle in, reminding me that these experiences were changing, and so was I.

As I stepped into the halls of Crossett High School for the final time, a sense of urgency hit me. This year felt like the turning point—my chance to stand out while everything around me was shifting. My classmates filled the space with loud conversations and easy excitement, but I still felt separate from it all. The pressure to perform stayed with me, pushing me forward while also making me question whether I was prepared for what was coming.

That feeling didn't have long to settle. A chance encounter with a coach started a chain of events that changed everything. One afternoon on the court, I came face to face with Coach Thompson, a seasoned mentor known for his steady presence. He carried himself with confidence that drew people in, and when he approached me, I felt a mix of anticipation and nerves.

Our conversation shifted quickly from small talk to discussions about potential, talent, and ambition. In that moment, I understood how much the future could change depending on what I did next. His words stirred something in me, pulling my passion for basketball back to the surface and pushing me toward a clearer sense of purpose. But when I spoke about wanting to make it to the NBA, I caught a brief hesitation in his expression. It was a quiet reminder of the obstacles ahead. A single moment of defiance later led to my removal from the basketball team, forcing me to reevaluate my goals and rethink the path I thought I would take.

In the weeks that followed, I committed myself fully to track and field, driven by the need to prove my potential in another arena. I trained relentlessly, each session strengthening my resolve. Day by day, I grew faster and more focused on the opportunities I still had. The support from my teammates energized me. We pushed one another, shared the highs and lows of practice, and carried a sense of unity that made the work feel meaningful. The intensity of training brought a new rhythm to my life, and I found myself thriving in it. I felt awake again, fully engaged with a passion that gave new direction to my goals.

Undeterred by setbacks, I chose to join the track team—a decision that would become a turning point in my journey. I didn't know it then, but this choice opened a door I hadn't even noticed. With every stride, I discovered a sense of freedom and clarity. The challenge was different: it demanded not just physical strength but also mental focus. Under the guidance of committed coaches, I honed my skills and developed a genuine passion for running, pushing myself to the edge of endurance.

The rhythm of my footsteps on the track became a measure of determination, each lap reinforcing my commitment and resolve. I grew to look forward to early morning practices and the wind rushing past as I sprinted the final stretch. In those moments, doubt fell away, replaced by a sense of purpose that drove me forward. The track became a space where I could focus entirely on the present. I began to recognize the parallels between basketball and running—the discipline, the focus, and the belief in one's own ability.

Both sports demanded everything I had, but they gave just as much in return. The challenges on the track mirrored those I had faced on the court, and with each day, my confidence grew. I was learning to trust my body again and to believe in my ability to adapt and overcome. Choosing a new path sparked a drive within me—a desire to excel and prove to myself that I could achieve greatness, despite past setbacks. This was not just about running; it was about reclaiming my identity and rewriting my story on my own terms.

The thrill of competition soon replaced the disappointment of lost dreams. I began to envision my future clearly, imagining myself on the podium, celebrating victory. I learned to channel the energy of past aspirations into my current pursuit, using the lessons from basketball to fuel my growing passion for track and field.

As the state track meet approached, I felt a mix of exhilaration and trepidation—a recognition that this was my chance to shine and leave a lasting mark in competition. The days leading up to the event were filled with anticipation, the excitement building as I prepared to showcase the results of my labor. I spent countless hours refining my technique, studying the competition, and mentally rehearsing each race, imagining myself crossing the finish line with arms raised in victory.

Yet with every heartbeat, the weight of expectation grew heavier, a reminder of the stakes involved. My dreams had evolved, taking on new dimensions, but my desire to succeed remained unchanged. I understood that this moment could redefine my narrative, offering a fresh start and a chance to leave behind the shadows of past failures. With the support of my coaches and teammates, a renewed sense of purpose coursed through me, drawing me ever closer to realizing my ambitions.

But fate had other plans, and a single moment would forever alter the trajectory of my life. The morning of the state track meet dawned crisp and clear, a reminder of the potential that awaited me. I could feel the energy in the air, the electric buzz of anticipation as athletes gathered, each fueled by dreams of glory. Yet just as I was ready to seize the moment, the unforeseen struck—a sudden injury during warmups, a split-second event that would reverberate through the halls of Crossett High School and beyond.

In an instant, everything changed. Chaos erupted, leaving me grappling with the reality of my shattered dreams. Panic rose within me, tears threatening to spill as I absorbed the magnitude of what had happened. My body had failed me when I needed it most, leaving me in confusion and despair. The dreams I had held so tightly now hung in the balance, suspended in the uncertainty of my future. As I was rushed to the sidelines, my heart ached under the weight of what could have been—a stark reminder that life has a way of testing our resolve when we least expect it.

In the days that followed, as I recovered from my injury, I grappled with a mixture of frustration, disappointment, and a profound sense of loss. The dreams I had pursued with such intensity now felt distant, as if slipping through my fingers like sand. I reflected on the path that had led me here—the countless hours of training, the sacrifices made, and the aspirations that had fueled my journey. Amidst the chaos of shattered dreams, however, I also discovered a newfound clarity.

The injury forced me to reevaluate my goals and confront the essence of what had driven me all along. I began to understand that while the pursuit of my dreams mattered, it was the journey itself—the friendships forged, the lessons learned, and the resilience developed—that held the deepest significance.

As I sat on the sidelines, watching my teammates compete, a surge of determination rose within me. While my body was sidelined, my spirit remained unbroken. I channeled that energy into supporting my teammates, cheering with unwavering enthusiasm and relishing their triumphs as if they were my own. In those moments, I found a new purpose—a realization that success can take many forms, and sometimes it is not about personal accolades but about lifting others along the way. I discovered the value of teamwork, the power of camaraderie, and the strength found in unity. It was in these moments of solidarity that I began to redefine success, embracing the idea that dreams can evolve into something different yet equally fulfilling.

With time, I learned to embrace the lessons hidden within my setback. I immersed myself in coaching, helping others refine their skills while rekindling my own love for the sport. I spent countless hours analyzing techniques, sharing knowledge with young athletes, and finding joy in their growth. The experience of injury had shifted my perspective, allowing me to appreciate the journey rather than focusing solely on the destination. I realized my dreams had not been extinguished; they had merely taken a different form, reflecting the resilience of the human spirit and the power of adaptation. The fire within me burned brightly once more, fueled by the desire to inspire others and to create a legacy beyond accolades.

As I stood on the sidelines of a track meet, watching young athletes push themselves to their limits, a sense of pride washed over me. The lessons I had learned through my journey had shaped me into a mentor, guiding the next generation toward their goals. I found fulfillment in celebrating their victories, recognizing that while my path may have veered off course, the passion that once drove me remained alive in the hearts of those I now inspired.

Each race they ran echoed my own aspirations, a reminder that the spirit of competition and the pursuit of dreams endure, transcending individual setbacks. I realized that while life may not always unfold as planned, the resilience of the human spirit allows us to redefine our dreams and embrace new possibilities. The laughter, camaraderie, and moments of triumph shared with my young athletes became the foundation of my new journey, each moment a reflection of hope and the potential that emerges when we dare to dream.

As the sun set on my high school years, I felt a profound sense of gratitude for the experiences that had shaped who I had become. The twists and turns of my journey had instilled a resilience that would serve me well in the years ahead. I carried the lessons learned, the friendships forged, and the memories created, each one forming a building block for my future. With a heart full of hope, I embraced the unknown, ready to forge my path in a world of possibilities.

As I stepped into the next chapter of my life, I knew that the dreams of my youth—though altered—would continue to guide me, lighting the way with the steady flame of hope.

CHAPTER 3

The Turning Point

"The human spirit is stronger than anything that can happen to it."

- C.C. Scott.

The days leading up to that fateful April 13, 1990, were thick with anticipation. It was as if the entire town, long accustomed to the monotony of daily life, held its collective breath for the dance at the youth center. For weeks, it had dominated conversations among my friends, classmates, and even the adults, who treated it as a major event. In our small, sleepy town, it was unusual for anything to happen, and the dance became a rare source of excitement in an otherwise predictable existence.

There was little to do in our corner of the world. If you weren't on a sports team or didn't have a close group of friends, your days could easily blur into a dull routine of school, home, and the occasional stop at our regular hangout, The Block. We went there to relax and enjoy music. It wasn't particularly exciting, but it was the only place where teens could sit for hours without being asked to leave.

For weeks leading up to the dance, every group in town prepared in its own way. The popular kids, those who always seemed effortlessly glamorous, floated through the hallways discussing their outfits in hushed voices, as if planning some exclusive event. There was talk of who was going with whom, which songs would play, and what kind of drama might unfold. For them, it wasn't just about dancing—it was about being seen. These were the same kids who dominated the social scene all year, but for some reason, this night carried a different weight. The undercurrent of competition buzzed through the air, and everyone felt it. Some were nervous, worried they wouldn't measure up, while others simply hoped they wouldn't trip or embarrass themselves in front of a crush.

In our small town, moments of excitement like this were rare, which made them all the more important. We didn't have malls to hang out in or movie theaters to escape to. The nearest big city was hours away, and most of us didn't even have cars. Any chance to break up the monotony was treasured. I could see it in the way my classmates' eyes lit up when they talked about the dance, as if it were a lifeline in an otherwise endless sea of sameness. We clung to these events not just for fun, but because they gave us something to look forward to— something that reminded us we were still young, still full of hope. For me, though, the excitement was tempered with something else, a feeling I couldn't shake. Deep down, I sensed this night would be different—not just memorable, but meaningful in a way I didn't yet understand.

The youth center dance had always been a yearly highlight, but this one felt different. There was an energy in the air that buzzed through the halls of the high school and spilled onto the streets. Excitement was contagious, pulling everyone into its orbit. It promised a night of freedom, a break from the rigid schedules and expectations that governed our lives. Even the teachers seemed to sense it, their usual stern expressions softening as they overheard our whispered plans between classes.

It's funny how a simple event can take on a life of its own, growing in importance until it feels like the culmination of something much bigger. I had never thought of the dance as more than a fun night out, a chance to laugh with friends. But this time, there was an electricity in the air I couldn't ignore. Everyone seemed to be counting down the days as if the dance were the pinnacle of high school, the one night where we could shed the labels that had defined us for so long. I found myself wondering what might happen if, just for once, we allowed ourselves to be different—bolder, freer, more honest. The jocks would still be jocks, and the popular girls would still reign supreme, but for a few hours, we would all be on equal footing, lost in the music and the energy of the night. It was a chance to rewrite the script, even if only for a little while.

The preparations had begun weeks in advance, with everyone at school obsessing over what to wear and who to go with. Excitement spread like wildfire, reaching even the teachers, who pretended not to care but secretly enjoyed the buzz as much as we did. Whispered conversations filled the halls—about secret crushes, who might ask whom to dance, and the kind of drama only high school can produce. Even the local radio station joined in, playing dance tunes and dedicating songs to people, we knew. It was all anyone could talk about, and I couldn't help but get swept up in it, even though I had my reservations.

There was a part of me that wondered why this dance felt so important. Was it because we were all desperate for something, anything, to break up the routine? Or was it because, deep down, we knew these fleeting nights of freedom and excitement would be the ones we remembered long after high school? Maybe it was both. In the end, it didn't matter. What mattered was that, for one night, we would all be united by a common goal: to have fun, to forget everything else, and to live in the moment. Even the quiet kids in the back of the classroom talked about what they would wear or who they might ask to dance. A shared buzz of anticipation filled the air, as if we were all holding our breath for something just out of reach. It wasn't about popularity or status anymore—it was about belonging, even if only for a few hours. And that meant everything to a group of teenagers trying to make sense of who they were.

As the date crept closer, I tried to hold onto that feeling, experiencing the buildup with a mixture of excitement and trepidation. The dance wasn't just a night out; it felt symbolic, though I couldn't quite explain why. It was a chance to shed the layers of my small-town identity and step into something bigger, something unknown. The event seemed to stretch across the horizon, imagined over and over in my mind, filled with possibilities and unspoken promises. Every song on the radio felt like the soundtrack to the night I was waiting for. I even caught myself practicing dance moves in front of the mirror, laughing at how silly I looked. But beneath the nerves was a quiet hope—that this night would be more than just another memory. It might be the beginning of something new.

In the days leading up to the dance, my mind spun with thoughts and emotions. I would lie awake at night, staring at the ceiling, imagining how the night might unfold. I pictured myself walking into the youth center, the music pounding through the walls, and, for once, feeling like I belonged. The dance was more than a fun night out. It felt like a test, a chance to prove something to myself, to the people who had known me all my life, and maybe even to the bullies who had made my life miserable. I wasn't sure what I wanted to prove—perhaps that I could rise above the labels and teasing, or that I could carve out a space for myself, independent of the roles everyone else had assigned.

There was a kind of magic in the anticipation, a sense that anything could happen. I imagined the possibilities: maybe I'd have a conversation with someone I had never spoken to before, sparking a friendship that could change my life. Maybe I'd finally work up the courage to dance with my crush, and they would see me in a different light. Or maybe I'd simply have a great time with my friends, laughing, dancing, and letting go of the worries that usually weighed me down. Whatever happened, I knew this night would be different, that it would stand out in my memory for years to come.

But fear was there too. What if the night didn't live up to the expectations I had built in my head? What if, instead of finding a sense of belonging, I was reminded of all the reasons I never quite fit in? What if the bullies saw it as another opportunity to humiliate me, to make sure I knew my place in the social hierarchy? The what-ifs circled in my mind, each one more anxiety-inducing than the last. I tried to shake them off, but they clung to me like shadows, growing darker as the night approached. Every glance in the hallway felt loaded, every snicker a possible insult. My heart raced at the thought of walking through the gym doors and facing a crowd that might still see me as the odd one out. Holding onto hope was difficult when fear kept whispering worst-case scenarios in my ear.

Despite these fears, part of me was determined to face whatever the night had in store. I had spent too many years hiding, trying to blend into the background, hoping the bullies would forget I existed. But they never did. No matter how much I tried to disappear, they always found me, always reminded me that I was different. Going to the dance felt like a declaration, a statement that I would no longer let them control my life. I wanted to prove, if only to myself, that I could show up without apology, that I had the right to be seen, to take up space, and to enjoy the night like everyone else. Even if things went wrong, even if I ended up embarrassed or hurt, at least I would have faced my fears head on. That, I realized, was more important than anything else.

Yet beneath my anticipation, there was an unease I couldn't shake. It was the weight of the past, the memories of a time when I couldn't move through the world with ease, when the bullies shadowing my every step turned even the simplest pleasures into an obstacle course of fear and humiliation. They had always lurked in the corners of my mind, casting a long shadow over my life. Their taunts echoed louder as the day approached, memories of their cruelty reawakening with an intensity that made my chest tighten. I flinched at old memories—hallway shoves, whispered insults—that had clung to me for years. Even though I had grown stronger and more self-assured, part of me still feared being dragged back into that darkness.

There's something about bullying that sticks with you long after the words have been said and the bruises have healed. The pain doesn't live only in the moments it happens—it follows you, like a shadow always present, just out of sight but never gone. Even when you think you've moved past it, even when you believe you've outgrown it, it can sneak up when you least expect it. A passing comment, a certain look, even the sound of someone's voice can bring it all rushing back, a flood of memories you thought were buried long ago. That was happening to me in the days leading up to the dance. The closer it got, the more I found myself haunted by the past.

The bullies in my life had been relentless. They weren't the kind who just made a snide comment and moved on. No, they took pleasure in tormenting me, finding new ways to make me feel small. It wasn't only physical intimidation, though there was plenty of that. It was the psychological warfare they waged, the way they made me second-guess myself at every turn. I walked through the halls with my head down, avoiding eye contact, never knowing when they might strike. Sometimes it was a shove into a locker; other times, an insult hurled across the cafeteria, loud enough for everyone to hear. Every day felt like a battle, and every victory, no matter how small, was hard earned.

The worst part was the way they made me feel powerless. No matter how much I tried to ignore them or stand up for myself, it never seemed to matter. They always found a way to get under my skin, to remind me that, in their eyes, I didn't belong. Over time, I started to believe them. Their words wormed into my mind, planting seeds of doubt that grew into a full-blown garden of insecurity. I began to see myself through their eyes, to believe I was everything they said I was—weak, unworthy, less than.

As the dance approached, those old insecurities bubbled to the surface. I had spent years rebuilding my sense of self, convincing myself that I wasn't defined by their cruelty. But the closer we got to the big night, the more those old wounds reopened. What if they were planning something? What if they saw this as their chance to strike again, to humiliate me in front of the entire school? The thought made my heart race and filled my stomach with a growing sense of dread.

In the weeks leading up to the dance, I tried to push these thoughts aside. I told myself this time would be different, that I had grown stronger, more resilient. But no matter how hard I tried to convince myself, the doubts lingered. The scars left by years of torment ran deep, and the thought of seeing them again—of potentially being cornered in that packed youth center—filled me with a dread I couldn't fully suppress.

It's strange how the mind works. You can spend years telling yourself you've moved on, that you've left the past behind, but all it takes is one small trigger, and suddenly you're right back in that place, feeling the old fears and insecurities as if no time has passed at all. That's what was happening to me. I had convinced myself I was ready, that I had grown since the last time the bullies tormented me. After all, it had been a while since they had actively targeted me. Maybe they had moved on, found someone else to pick on. Or maybe they had simply grown bored. But deep down, I knew that wasn't true. Bullies don't stop because they get bored. They stop when they've done enough damage—and I wasn't sure if they were done with me yet.

Every time I thought about walking into that dance, I imagined the worst-case scenario. I pictured them waiting at the entrance, smirking as they plotted their next move. I saw myself tripping over my own feet, spilling punch on my clothes, and becoming the laughingstock of the night. I envisioned them cornering me, saying something so cruel I would be left speechless, unable to defend myself. These thoughts swirled in my mind, making it hard to focus on anything else.

But then I reminded myself how far I had come. I had survived their bullying before, and I could survive it again. I wasn't the same scared kid they used to torment. I had grown tougher, more resilient. I had learned how to stand up for myself, even if it wasn't always easy. Most importantly, I had people in my life who cared about me—friends who had my back, who wouldn't let me face the bullies alone. I wasn't going to let fear hold me back this time. I was going to the dance, no matter what.

As the day of the dance approached, I felt a mix of

excitement and dread swirling inside me, like a storm brewing just beneath the surface. I could almost hear the music playing in my head, imagine the laughter and joy that would fill the air, yet the shadows of my past loomed large, threatening to overshadow those moments. I took a deep breath, reminding myself that this was my chance to rewrite the narrative, to step into the light instead of retreating into the darkness of my fears.

The dance was meant to be a night of escape, a brief reprieve from the mundane, but the closer it got, the more it felt like a battlefield. A place where I would have to confront my demons, not just in my mind but in the flesh. Yet despite the fear, despite the persistent unease, I made the decision to go. It wasn't just about the dance—it was about reclaiming a part of myself lost to years of bullying and fear.

With each passing hour, the weight of anticipation pressed down on me, but a flicker of hope ignited within. I imagined stepping onto the dance floor, surrounded by friends who believed in me, their laughter drowning out the echoes of past taunts. I pictured myself dancing freely, letting the rhythm wash over me, each beating a step toward liberation. This was my moment to shine, to show not just the bullies but also myself that I was no longer defined by their cruelty.

There was something empowering about deciding to go, even though I was terrified. By making that choice, I was telling the bullies—and myself—that they no longer controlled me. Over the years, they had taken so much: my confidence, my sense of safety, my ability to enjoy life without constantly looking over my shoulder. But this was one thing they could not take. The dance was meant to be a night of fun, a night of celebration, and I was determined to enjoy it, no matter what happened.

In a way, the dance represented more than just a social event. It was a chance to reclaim something I had lost, something intangible but vital. I had spent so much time living in fear, constantly worrying about what the bullies might do or say. This time, I was choosing to face that fear head on. I knew it would not be easy, and I knew things might not go as I hoped, but I also knew I had to try. If I let fear dictate my life, I would never be free.

The decision to go to the dance was not just about proving something to the bullies—it was about proving something to myself. I had spent so much time doubting my own strength, my own worth. The bullies had made me question everything, and for a long time, I had believed their lies. But now I was ready to take back control. I was ready to show myself that I was stronger than I had ever realized.

When the night finally arrived, the atmosphere in town was electric, buzzing with energy. The streets were filled with teenagers dressed in their finest—the girls in bright skirts and sparkly tops, the boys in button-up shirts and stylish slacks that fit their growing frames. I could hear the hum of excitement as I made my way to the youth center, my heart pounding like a drum. It felt as though the entire town had turned out for the event, everyone eager for a night of distraction from the dull grind of small-town life.

The town came alive for events like this, shifting from its usual quiet rhythm into something vibrant and full of energy. Normally, it was the kind of place where everyone knew each other, and nothing much ever happened. But on nights like this, it felt as if the whole town had woken up, shaking off the monotony of everyday life to embrace something special. The streets were lined with cars, their headlights cutting through the darkness, while groups of teenagers made their way to the youth center. Laughter and conversation filled the air, the sound of anticipation building with each step, and for the first time in a long while, I felt the weight of my fears begin to lift, replaced by a sense of belonging I had longed for.

The energy of the night buzzed around me as I walked, my hands trembling slightly with a mix of nerves and excitement. My friends were already at the entrance, faces lit up by the thrill of the night. They had been talking about this dance for weeks, and now that it was finally here, they were ready to make the most of it. I could see the excitement in their eyes, the way they looked at each other with wide smiles, as if they could hardly believe the night had finally arrived.

As I approached the youth center, a surge of optimism ran through me. Maybe tonight would be different. Maybe the bullies wouldn't even notice me. Maybe I could blend into the crowd, lose myself in the music, the laughter, and the energy of the night. The thought gave me a brief sense of peace, and for a moment, I allowed myself to believe that everything could be okay.

But the closer I got to the building, the tighter the familiar knot of anxiety became in my stomach. The youth center loomed ahead, its lights glowing in the darkness. Inside, I knew, were the bullies, waiting for their chance. I could almost feel their eyes on me already, even before stepping through the doors. The fear was there, simmering beneath the surface, but I pushed it down. I had made my decision. I was going to face whatever came my way.

The youth center was buzzing when I arrived. Music blared from inside, muffled slightly by the thick walls but loud enough to make the bass vibrate beneath my feet. Lights spilled out onto the sidewalk, illuminating the faces of kids gathered outside, laughing and chatting excitedly.

Tonight felt different. There was an edge to the excitement, a tension that made the air thick with possibility. I could see it in the way people moved, swaying slightly to the music as they stood outside, waiting to go in. I could hear it in their voices, filled with nervous energy as they laughed and joked. Everyone was on edge, waiting for something to happen, though no one knew exactly what.

As I approached the door, a wave of panic rose in my chest. What if they were waiting for me inside, ready the moment I stepped through? What if they had planned something worse than anything before? The thoughts raced through my mind, each one more terrifying than the last. But I couldn't turn back. I had come this far, and fear was not going to stop me.

Taking a deep breath, I stepped through the door. The music hit me like a wave, filling the air and vibrating through my body. The youth center was packed, kids dancing and laughing, the lights flashing in time with the beat. It was chaotic but in a good way—a-controlled chaos that made everything feel alive, as if the night itself pulsed with energy.

For a moment, I stood at the entrance, trying to get my bearings. The room was dimly lit, the flashing lights casting long shadows on the walls. I scanned the crowd, looking for any sign of the bullies, but I didn't see them. Maybe they weren't here yet, or maybe they were lost in the crowd, blending in. Either way, a small sense of relief washed over me. Maybe tonight would be different.

I made my way toward my friends near the punch bowl, laughing and talking animatedly. They waved when they saw me, their faces lighting up with excitement. It was clear they were already enjoying the night, and for a moment, I allowed myself to relax. The music was loud, the atmosphere electric, and for the first time in a long time, I felt like I could just enjoy the night.

As I joined my friends, I couldn't shake the feeling that something was about to happen—a sense of foreboding that hovered over me like a shadow. The unease that had been simmering all day remained, a constant reminder that the bullies could strike at any moment, lurking just out of sight. I tried to push the thoughts aside, to focus on the music, the laughter, and the energy of the night, but it was difficult. Every time someone brushed past me, I flinched, half expecting it to be one of them, ready to make their move, their laughter echoing in my mind.

Despite my efforts to stay calm, the fear persisted, gnawing at the edges of my thoughts like a persistent itch I couldn't scratch. It hung over me like a dark cloud, threatening to ruin the night before it had even begun. I wanted to believe that everything would be fine, that I could enjoy the dance like everyone else, but the sense that something bad was coming refused to fade. I glanced at my friends, their faces bright with joy, and felt a pang of guilt for not fully immersing myself in the moment. I longed to let go of my worries, to dance freely without the weight of anxiety pressing down, but the fear felt like an anchor, holding me back from the joy around me.

CHAPTER 4

The Night of the Incident

"In the midst of darkness, there is always light. In the depths of despair, there is always hope. And in the face of adversity, there is always the opportunity for redemption."

The pulsating rhythm of the music filled the air, creating a tangible sense of excitement and anticipation. It was Friday April 13, 1990, a date that would forever remain etched in my memory—the night everything changed. As I stepped into the Youth Center, a mix of nerves and exhilaration coursed through me. The promise of a few hours of freedom from the pressures of small-town life drew me onto the dance floor, where I hoped to lose myself in the music and, if only for a moment, forget the weight of my troubles.

As the night went on, the Youth Center shifted from a haven of excitement to a battleground for my inner demons. The flickering lights and pulsing music offered a temporary reprieve, but beneath the surface, the shadows of my past loomed, threatening to break the fragile facade of happiness.

The bullies, circling like vultures, seemed to appear from

nowhere, their presence thickening the air with tension. Their mocking laughter and taunts cut through the room, each barbing a sharp reminder of the torment I had endured for so long. Despite my attempts to ignore them, their harassment persisted, chipping away at my resolve and eroding my fragile sense of self-worth.

With each passing moment, the weight of their words grew heavier, dragging me deeper into despair. I felt trapped, confined by walls that seemed to close in with every breath. Desperation clawed at my chest, urging me to escape the suffocating grip of my tormentors.

Then, like a spark setting off a powder keg, a confrontation erupted, shattering the fragile calm of the dance. It began with muttered insults and a careless shove, and before I knew it, tempers flared and fists flew. The air crackled with tension as the fight escalated, each blow fueling anger and drawing the attention of everyone around us.

In the heat of the moment, I found myself caught in the crossfire, a pawn in a game of violence and retribution, my heart racing as I tried to make sense of the chaos. Adrenaline surged through my veins, drowning out reason and propelling me into the heart of the fray, where fear and confusion ruled. It was a blur of motion and emotion, a chaotic symphony of rage and fear that crescendo with the deafening roar of gunfire, a sound slicing through the night.

The noise reverberated through the air, a thunderous reminder of life's fragility and the consequences of violence, sending shockwaves of panic through the crowd. Time seemed to stand still as the echoes of gunfire faded, leaving behind a trail of devastation. I saw the faces of my friends, expressions frozen in horror, mirroring my own disbelief. In that moment, the dance shifted from celebration to nightmare, and I realized that the safety I had sought was now a distant memory, replaced by a chilling uncertainty that gripped my heart.

As the dust settled and the gravity of the night sank in, a profound emptiness washed over me. I was shaken to the core, my spirit bruised and battered by the events of that fateful evening. Yet amid the chaos, a flicker of hope emerged—a determination to rise from the ashes of adversity and embrace the second chance I had been given.

Though the road ahead was uncertain, I knew I would not walk it alone. Even in the darkest times, the human spirit possesses a remarkable capacity to endure, carrying me through the trials ahead.

The impact hit like a sledgehammer to the chest, knocking the wind out of me and sending me crashing to the ground. Pain seared through my body, white hot and all-consuming, as I lay bleeding on the cold pavement. The world around me blurred and faded, replaced by numbness and disbelief, as if I were watching everything unfold from a distance, detached from my own reality.

In that moment, time stretched into eternity, each passing second an agonizing reminder of pain and uncertainty. I struggled to make sense of what had happened, my mind reeling from the shock of the gunshot wounds now marking my body. It was as if I had been thrust into a nightmare with no escape—a nightmare where the line between reality and fantasy blurred into an indistinct haze. I felt the warmth of my blood pooling beneath me, a stark contrast to the cold pavement, and wondered if this was how it all ended.

As I lay there, my senses dulled by pain, I heard the frantic shouts and cries around me, their voices rising in a chorus of panic and fear. The world spun in dizzying circles, the cacophony echoing in my ears like a symphony of chaos. I tried to focus, to hold on to the thread of consciousness tethering me to reality, but it slipped through my fingers like grains of sand. Faces loomed above me, distorted and blurred, their expressions a mix of horror and urgency, but I could not make out their words—only the frantic intensity in their voices.

In that moment, I felt a profound sense of isolation, as if I were trapped in a bubble, separated from the chaos around me. I wanted to scream, to tell them I was still here, still fighting, but the words would not come. Instead, I felt myself drifting, the edges of my vision darkening as the world slipped further away. Just as I thought I might fall into oblivion, a voice broke through the haze, calling my name and grounding me in the reality of my pain and the fight for my life.

I had been shot—once in the head, with the bullet passing through my neck (a fragment from the gun is still lodged there), once in the lower abdomen, and once in the lower pelvis. The severity of my injuries was staggering, the damage undeniable. My head and stomach swelled, stark reminders of the violence inflicted on me. Tubes ran in and out of my body, connecting me to machines that beeped and whirred with mechanical precision.

Here are my x rays that clearly show the damage:

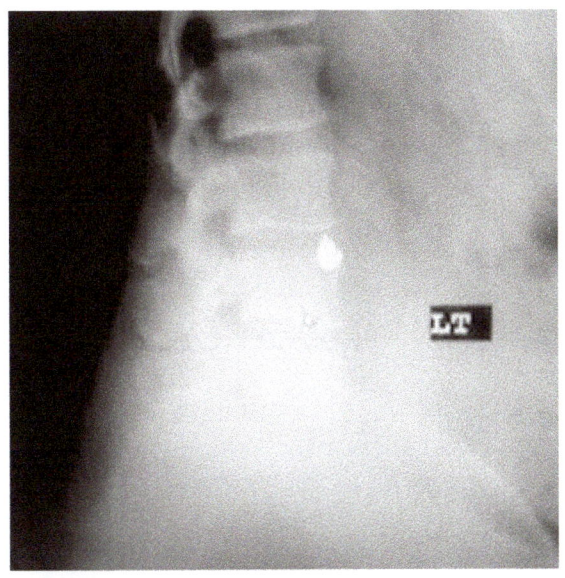

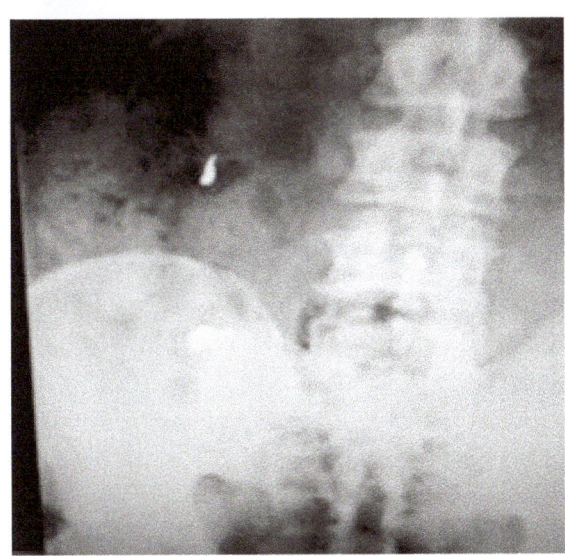

Each breath I took was a struggle, the air burning in my lungs as I fought to stay conscious. The pain was relentless, pressing in on me with a force that felt ready to pull me under. Yet, in the middle of the agony and rising despair, a small surge of determination pushed through—a quiet but steady refusal to let go of life.

It became a fight balanced on the edge of survival, where every heartbeat marked another moment kept away from the darkness trying to swallow me. I held on to that small spark of hope with everything I had, refusing to give in to the sense of defeat gathering around me like a storm. As long as breath still moved through my chest, I knew there was a chance—a chance to outlast this moment, to rise again, to claim my story instead of being overtaken by it.

So, I kept fighting. I fought against the pain burning through me, against the fear that tried to seep into my thoughts, and against the pull of hopelessness that pressed at me like an anchor. Slowly, almost imperceptibly, something shifted. A bit of light broke through the darkness—unsteady at first, but real enough to reach.

It was a long and demanding journey, filled with setbacks and challenges that felt impossible to navigate at times. Each day brought new obstacles and moments when I wanted to stop trying, but I refused to let those moments define me. With the help and support of my family and friends, I found the strength to keep going, to push through the pain, and to accept the second chance I had been given. Their steady belief in my ability to recover fueled my determination and reminded me that I was not facing this alone.

As I rose from that deep place of despair, worn down but steady, I understood that I had been given something rare—a life renewed in the middle of adversity. Gratitude settled in with every breath and every experience that still reached me. The world felt sharper, the sounds clearer, and I realized I was seeing life from a different angle. I was not only a survivor; I was someone prepared to face what came next with resilience and intent.

The prognosis was grim. I was in critical condition, balanced between life and death. Even as the doctors worked with everything they had to save me, nothing was certain. My family prepared themselves for the worst, holding on to hope as tightly as they could.

In the sterile confines of the hospital room, I lay surrounded by wires and tubes, each beep from the machines a sharp reminder of how fragile life can be. The scent of antiseptic filled the air and blended with the quiet prayers of loved ones gathered at my bedside, their faces tight with worry and fear.

Yet, against all odds, I began to fight. In that dim room, with machines humming around me and whispered prayers close by, I found the strength to push back against the pull of death. Every breath felt like a small step away from the darkness that pressed in on me.

The road to recovery was long and demanding, marked by setbacks that made progress feel unpredictable. Some days the pain was so intense that stopping felt easier than continuing, as if the weight of my injuries were pressing down on me, making it hard to move forward.

But through it all, I held on to hope, refusing to give in to the despair that tried to pull me under. With each passing day, I felt strength returning to my body—slow, steady, and noticeable enough to keep me fighting.

The path forward was uncertain, and the outcome often felt unclear. Still, with the support of my family and friends, I found the courage to continue, to push through the pain, and to accept the second chance I had been given.

As days turned into weeks and weeks into months, I watched my body begin to recover. Each small improvement reinforced my resilience. The swelling in my head and stomach eased, and the pain shifted into a quiet ache that stayed in the background, a reminder of how far I had come. I found myself in awe of what the human body can repair, even after severe trauma, and I felt a renewed sense of appreciation for life.

But the scars, both physical and emotional, remained. They were constant reminders of what I had survived. Each mark on my skin carried a story, a chapter of endurance I would always hold with me. Instead of weighing me down, they became markers of strength—signs of the battles I had faced and the progress I had made. I came to understand that these scars were more than reminders of pain. They were signs of resilience, proof that I had faced darkness and found my way back.

When I finally stepped out of that hospital room, worn down but still standing, I knew I had been given a rare gift. Life felt renewed in a way I had never experienced. My first steps outside, with the sun warming my face, felt like a beginning. The road ahead was still uncertain, but I walked forward with intention, ready for whatever came next. I wanted to live fully, appreciate every moment, and acknowledge the journey that had shaped me. With each step, a sense of purpose grew stronger—a steady urge to inspire others who might be fighting their own battles. I was no longer only a survivor; I had become a source of hope, ready to share my story and encourage others to find their strength.

It was a slow and exhausting process, filled with frustration, pain, and moments of despair that felt overwhelming. Learning to walk again, to talk again, and to read, write, and think felt like trying to climb a mountain with lead weights strapped to my limbs. Every task became a challenge. Each step forward came with aching muscles and trembling limbs. Every word I managed to say was a fight against the fog that clouded my mind, making even simple conversations feel like climbing a steep hill.

But with every small victory, no matter how insignificant it seemed, hope began to rise in me again. It sparked a strength that had been silent for a long time. It reminded me that even in the hardest moments, there was room for progress and renewal. I started to celebrate the little things: the first time I stood without help, the moment I formed a full sentence, and the relief of reading a paragraph without losing my place. Each achievement, even the smallest one, became a stepping stone on my path to recovery.

I was a survivor, and I was determined to make the most of the second chance I had been given. With steady resolve and a clear sense of purpose, I committed myself to the demanding work of rehabilitation, pushing my body and mind toward recovery. I stayed close to friends and family whose support fueled my determination. I learned to accept the struggle, realizing that every setback carried the potential for a return. With each day, I grew stronger, more resilient, and more aware of the strength within me to face difficult challenges.

Physical therapy became my daily ritual, a disciplined routine designed to rebuild my strength, mobility, and coordination. Each session tested my endurance and forced me to work through pain and exhaustion. Still, day after day, I felt myself growing more capable and more determined to rise above the obstacles in front of me.

As my body began to heal, my mind did the same, slowly gathering itself after the damage, forming a clearer sense of who I was now. Speech therapy helped me reclaim the words taken from me when the bullet passed through my skull. Each syllable felt like a small step away from silence. I remember the first time I spoke a full sentence; it felt like a declaration that I was still here. Reading and writing, once routine, became major milestones in my recovery and gave me a renewed sense of purpose.

The hardest part was learning to manage the surge of emotions that came with the trauma. It often felt like a storm moving through me. The memory of the shooting stayed close, casting a shadow over moments that should have brought relief or joy, making it difficult to fully settle into the present. Fear, anger, and grief competed for space in my mind, pulling at my focus and feeding doubt. I spent many days wrestling with these feelings, trying to understand how they fit into my healing, and the effort often left me exhausted.

Yet even in the middle of the darkness, there were moments of light—brief reminders of how precious life still was. The laughter of loved ones, the warmth of the sun on my face, and the quiet of being alone for a moment reminded me that despite everything, there was still beauty in the world. I learned to appreciate these moments and hold on to them because they helped steady me when everything else felt uncertain.

I kept moving forward, driven by a determination that refused to fade. Each day brought new challenges and new setbacks, but each one also created space for progress. I started seeing my recovery not only as a struggle but as evidence of the strength people can bring out of themselves when they have no other choice.

I was a survivor, rising from adversity stronger than before. I accepted my scars, both the ones I could see and the ones I couldn't, as parts of my story and reminders of the battles I had fought through. The road ahead was still long and unpredictable, but I faced it with a lifted head, ready for whatever came next. I understood that no matter what waited for me, I had already beaten the hardest challenge—reclaiming my life after the tragedy. And I was committed to making every moment that followed count.

CHAPTER 5

The Road to Recovery

"In the midst of adversity, one discovers the true strength of the human spirit." - **Dalai Lama.**

As I grappled with my initial difficulties, I found myself facing a daunting line of challenges. Tasks I once completed without thought now felt impossible. I had always taken pride in being self-sufficient and moving through life with ease, but after the trauma, everything shifted. Even the most ordinary activities felt like a climb I wasn't prepared for. The frustrations of each day ran deep. Brushing my teeth felt like running a marathon where the starting line was unclear, and the finish line hardly existed. Every muscle resisted the simplest actions, as if it had forgotten what to do.

The sense of betrayal from my own body was overwhelming. Each failed attempt to tie my shoes reminded me that returning to any form of normalcy would take time. The mental fog made the process even harder. My thoughts scattered so easily that forming a complete idea felt like work. I often caught myself staring into the distance, stuck in a space that didn't make sense. The world, once predictable, felt unfamiliar. Sounds were sharp, and bright lights felt aggressive, adding to the constant sense of overload. It was as if my entire system had been reset, leaving me to navigate a reality I didn't recognize. The uncertainty forced me to search for strength I never knew I had.

Reading, once a source of joy and escape, became an exercise in frustration as I struggled to make sense of the words on the page. Writing felt just as unreachable. My hand trembled with the effort it took to form even the simplest letters. Words that had once been my sanctuary now felt distant, slipping away as if written in a code I could no longer understand. I would sit down with a book hoping to disappear into the story, but the letters never settled. They shifted and blurred until the page became a field of shapes with no meaning. Something I had cherished all my life had turned into a task that drained me.

My mind, once quick and reliable, now moved slowly. Focusing on a single paragraph took effort I didn't expect. Writing only deepened the disappointment. Holding a pen felt unfamiliar; my hand shook, and the letters that once came easily showed up uneven and distorted. The stories I used to devour now read like an undecipherable puzzle. Each sentence felt like a structure I couldn't navigate, and I lost my place before I had even found it. It felt like a harsh twist of fate, as if the tools I once depended on to make sense of my world were now refusing to respond. My once active thoughts had been replaced with a dull hum that made me question myself constantly. This struggle with words was a steady reminder of how much had shifted, cutting into a part of my identity I had always trusted. At times, the frustration broke through, and the tears came—not only for the abilities I had lost, but for the crushing sense that my connection to myself was fading, letter by letter.

When people hear the word "recovery," they may think of

recovering from alcohol or drug use. While that is one interpretation, recovery is a universal concept representing a return to a stable state of health and well-being. For me, recovery meant reclaiming my life, step by agonizing step. It was not just about healing the physical wounds that had left me battered; it was about piecing together the fragments of my soul. Recovery involved rediscovering the person I had been and, more importantly, learning to accept and embrace the person I was becoming. The word "recovery" suggests finality, as if once the process is complete, everything will return to the way it once was. My journey taught me that recovery is anything but a destination. It is an ongoing, evolving process. It required accepting that I would never be exactly who I had been but that I had the opportunity to become stronger, more capable, and more resilient.

This process of change helped me move toward my fullest potential and a renewed sense of purpose and value. In the beginning, it felt as though I was merely surviving, navigating the relentless stream of challenges that confronted me. Over time, I began to see that these difficulties, painful as they were, were shaping me into a new version of myself. There was power in this transformation, even if I could not perceive it at first. With each day, I moved beyond mere survival toward something more meaningful—something that gave my life a deeper sense of purpose. Each small victory, each incremental step toward regaining control, became not just a reflection of my physical and mental endurance but a reclamation of my sense of value.

I began to notice small improvements, like finally managing to tie my shoes or read a full paragraph, and I recognized them as huge accomplishments. These moments, no matter how minor, ignited a spark of hope that had been absent for so long. It felt as though I was slowly piecing myself back together, bit by painful bit. The resilience I discovered surprised me, revealing that I was stronger than I had ever imagined. This new strength was not about avoiding pain but about learning to live with it and still move forward. In this process, I learned that purpose is not a destination but a continuous path of growth, one fueled by perseverance and nurtured by hope. Each challenge, each obstacle, was not a setback but a building block toward becoming the most authentic version of myself.

Walking, once a natural and effortless act, now demanded near impossible effort. Each step was a battle against gravity and the pain radiating through my battered body. I had never truly appreciated the miracle of walking before. It was something I had always done without thought, a function so deeply embedded in my consciousness it had felt as natural as breathing. After the trauma, every step felt like climbing a mountain. The automatic motion of placing one foot in front of the other had become an exercise in endurance and sheer will. My legs, which had carried me so confidently through life, now trembled under the strain, as if rebelling against their very purpose. Pain surged with every movement, relentless and searing, radiating from my core outward like fire. Each step became a negotiation with my body, a careful calculation of how far I could push before the pain became overwhelming. Even shuffling across a room felt like an epic journey, leaving me breathless and aching. My mind would often scream at my legs to move, but they simply would not cooperate. The world felt heavier, the ground beneath me unyielding and unforgiving. Yet in those moments of struggle, I realized that each step—no matter how painful—was a step toward reclaiming my independence. It was proof that, though my body had been broken, my spirit remained whole.

Talking, too, was its own challenge. Words tumbled from my lips in a jumble, my tongue tripping over syllables and sounds as I struggled to articulate my thoughts. Conversations, once a source of connection and comfort, had become battlegrounds of frustration. The words that had once flowed so easily now felt trapped, tangled in the aftermath of trauma and recovery. My tongue, once fluid and agile, now felt heavy and sluggish, weighed down by the enormity of my experiences. I often paused, searching for the right words, only to watch them dissolve before I could grasp them. It was like trying to catch smoke—the harder I tried, the more elusive they became. There were moments when I felt I had lost not only my voice but also my ability to connect with the world around me. Simple exchanges—asking for a glass of water or responding to a greeting—became monumental tasks that left me exhausted. Every conversation reminded me of how far I still had to go. The silence that followed my fumbled attempts at speech was deafening, amplifying my sense of isolation. I longed to express the swirling thoughts and emotions inside me, but the bridge between my mind and my mouth seemed to have crumbled. Yet even in those moments of struggle, a growing determination emerged—to reclaim my voice and speak my truth with clarity and strength, no matter how long it took.

Even as I faced these daunting challenges, I refused to surrender to despair. Each day, I summoned the strength to push forward, confront my limitations, and reclaim control over my destiny. Despair lurked at the edges of my consciousness, whispering in moments of weakness. There were days when the weight of my struggles threatened to crush me, when the pain and frustration seemed too much to bear. Yet deep inside, a flicker of something stronger refused to be extinguished. It was a fierce determination born of the belief that my limitations did not define me. I was not my pain, my trauma, or my struggles. I was more than the sum of my suffering. Day by day, I made the choice to confront my challenges with courage and resolve. I refused to let my circumstances dictate the course of my life. Slowly but surely, I began to reclaim my sense of control and take back the reins of my destiny from the hands of despair.

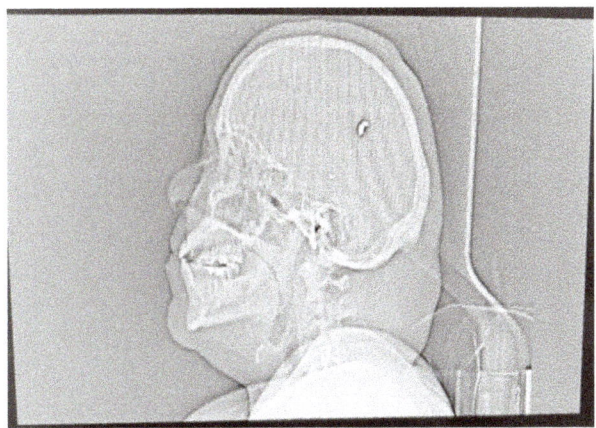

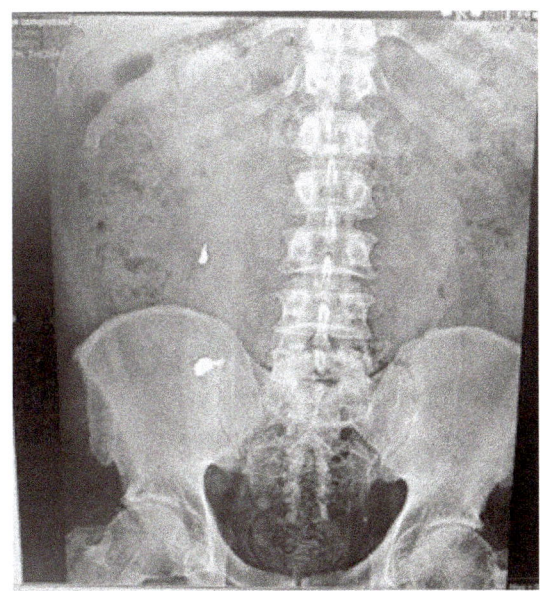

CHAPTER 6

Educational Journey

"Education is the most powerful weapon which you can use to change the world." **– Nelson Mandela.**

Graduating from high school is a milestone for many, but for me, it was evidence of sheer determination and resilience. After the life altering events of Friday, the 13th, 1990, returning to the classroom was not just a challenge. It was a battle that tested my physical, mental, and emotional limits. The gunshot wounds left me with significant physical and cognitive impairments, and each day brought a new hurdle I had to face.

I had to relearn basic skills such as reading, writing, and speaking—skills most people never question. The process was slow and filled with obstacles. Each day in high school felt like a marathon that stretched my endurance and patience. I often sat in class staring at the blackboard, the words blurring together like a puzzle that refused to form a clear picture. The classroom, once a place of learning and laughter, became a battleground where I fought against my own body and mind.

The challenges I faced reached far beyond academics; they affected every part of my daily life and forced me to rebuild myself piece by piece. Recovery was not linear, and setbacks were common, testing my resolve at every turn. There were moments when progress felt impossibly slow, yet each small achievement sparked hope that I held onto with everything I had.

The memories of that day stayed with me—the sharp sounds of chaos, the confusion, the screams, and the fear that hit without warning. It was not only the physical scars that followed me. The emotional weight ran deeper and lingered in ways I did not expect. I felt isolated, caught between inadequacy and a sense of loss that was hard to name. Sitting in a classroom became its own challenge. Being surrounded by my peers reminded me of everything I had survived and everything I felt I no longer fit into. I often felt like an observer watching life from the outside.

My friends moved through school with a confidence I no longer had. Their conversations about prom, college applications, and weekend plans felt distant, as if I were listening through a wall. While they planned for their futures, I focused on something far more immediate—making it through each lesson without feeling overwhelmed. Each day carried the weight of my past, a shadow that followed me everywhere and reminded me how uncertain everything felt. I missed the easy days of being young when friendships were simple and worries were light. At the same time, I began to realize that my path would not mirror anyone else's. That understanding, although difficult, pushed me toward a quieter kind of strength. I started to see that vulnerability could connect people, even when fear tried to push them apart. That shift helped me reach for relationships again, even when it felt risky.

Simple tasks like taking notes or joining class discussions became daunting, and my confidence dropped. My fingers struggled to keep up with my thoughts, and at times the words I wanted to say slipped away, leaving me frustrated and embarrassed. My mind moved fast, but my body lagged, creating a gap that felt impossible to close. Even with these challenges, I was fortunate to have teachers and classmates who understood what I was facing. Their support became essential, especially when school felt overwhelming.

They often stepped in with patience, guidance, and encouragement that helped me keep going. I remember my English teacher, Mrs. Thompson, who stayed with me after class and worked through grammar and composition at a pace that made sense for me. I spent hours in her classroom, using the extra resources she prepared and asking questions I never felt comfortable asking anywhere else. Those quiet sessions offered more than academic help. They gave me a place where I could admit my fears and talk about what I hoped for, without feeling judged. Her belief in me sparked a small sense of hope and reminded me that I was not defined by my limitations. Over time, I began to see that my journey was not only about getting past obstacles. It was also about finding out what I could do, what I cared about, and what strengths were waiting beneath the struggle. These moments strengthened my academic skills and helped me feel a sense of belonging I had been missing.

The school's administration played an essential role in supporting my needs. They gave me access to special education resources and adjusted my coursework to match my pace. The educational support services team worked consistently to make sure I had what I needed to move forward. This support helped me participate in a way that felt fair and gave me a real chance to progress. I used assistive technology that made reading and writing more manageable, and it reminded me that I wasn't doing this alone. My teachers became strong advocates for me, often updating my parents about how I was doing and where I was struggling. They encouraged me to speak up about what I needed and helped me understand the value of advocating for myself—something that would matter even more later in life.

Even with all of this support, there were moments when frustration took over. I often felt isolated, trying to keep up both academically and socially. I watched my friends excel, talking about weekend plans and future goals, while I struggled to grasp basic ideas. Their conversations felt distant, like something happening just out of reach. While they were planning college tours and thinking ahead, I was focused on getting through each class without feeling overwhelmed. I remember sitting in the lunchroom, surrounded by laughter and chatter, feeling like a ghost drifting through a world I no longer felt connected to. The energy around me contrasted with my internal struggle, which only amplified my sense of distance. My peers talked about the latest trends, upcoming events, and their dreams of adulthood while I stayed anchored to my past, weighed down by memories that refused to fade. Still, every obstacle eventually became a steppingstone. Each one pushed me to build resilience and adapt, even when it felt uncomfortable.

I began to see that these challenges, as painful as they were, carried lessons about who I was and what I could handle. Perseverance stopped being an idea and became a skill I had to practice daily. Every small victory—understanding a difficult math problem or delivering a presentation with confidence—felt like a personal breakthrough. These moments, no matter how small, reminded me that I was capable of progress. They fueled my determination to keep moving forward.

High school graduation was only the beginning. Enrolling in college introduced a new wave of challenges, and the reality of higher education felt like a steep climb. I was determined to continue my education, but the road ahead came with real obstacles. The transition from high school to college is difficult for any student, but my path carried its own weight. When I stepped onto the college campus for the first time, I was struck by its size and the range of people who filled it. Students from different places and backgrounds moved through the space with purpose. The atmosphere carried a sense of drive, but I also felt a rise of anxiety. I had worked hard to reach that moment, yet part of me questioned whether I was prepared. I felt like an outsider in a place filled with capable students, unsure if I could keep up with what college would demand.

The first major challenge was getting admitted. My high school grades were inconsistent, reflecting the struggles I faced. The application process was overwhelming; the forms, essays, and deadlines created a heavy sense of pressure. Still, my persistence and the story of my recovery stood out to the admissions team. I put genuine effort into the application, sharing not only my academic path but also the experiences that shaped me. I wanted to express the grit and persistence that shaped my journey, knowing my story might resonate with others.

I wrote about my challenges, the progress I made, and the steady hope that pushed me toward education. I focused on how those experiences shaped my values, mindset, and goals. I was admitted to a college that looked beyond grades and acknowledged the human effort behind each application. They recognized potential in students who kept going despite setbacks. Receiving the acceptance letter was a moment of real validation. It meant someone else saw the possibility in me. It marked the start of a chapter I had worked hard to reach.

Once I started college, the effort required to earn a degree increased. Academic expectations were higher, and competition was intense. My physical limitations continued to create real obstacles. Taking clear notes, completing lab work, and keeping up with long reading assignments required consistent effort and often left me drained. I realized quickly that my cognitive challenges became even more noticeable in the college environment. I struggled to stay focused during lectures, drifting as I tried to understand complex theories. The pressure was heavy, and I often felt like I was pushing against resistance. Many nights were spent in the library, surrounded by books and pages of notes, carrying the weight of everything I wanted to achieve. The nights slipped into early mornings as I fought fatigue, trying to absorb information while managing the doubts that pushed at my focus.

The academic workload felt like a steady climb, and I questioned whether I had the stamina to continue. Still, I kept showing up—class after class, assignment after assignment. Each completed task became a quiet win. I reminded myself that I had already faced harder battles, and this was another step in the process. Campus support services, including tutoring centers and disability accommodations, became essential resources. I no longer saw asking for help as a weakness. It was a decision based on clarity and strategy. What sustained me was the picture of a better future—the kind of future education could open.

Financial strain added another layer of difficulty. The cost of college was heavy, and I had to juggle part time jobs with my coursework. Scholarships and financial aid helped, though they didn't always cover everything. I remember the long hours working in a local café, where I served coffee while learning useful lessons in time management and communication. The café became a familiar space, filled with the smell of pastries and the steady rhythm of conversations. It offered a brief break from academic pressure.

Some nights, after a closing shift, I went straight to the library—tired but committed. Each shift reinforced my resolve, teaching me how to balance competing demands and build a consistent work ethic. There were days when I questioned whether I could keep going, but I always found a reason to push through. My coworkers became part of my support system, offering encouragement during tough times. That period taught me how to handle stress and stay composed even when things felt overwhelming. Despite everything, I remained focused on my goal. I surrounded myself with motivational quotes and reminders of why I had chosen this path. I pictured the future I wanted and used that image to keep myself moving. Whenever I felt close to giving up, I would close my eyes and remind myself how far I had come and how much further I still planned to go. Every step, even the small ones, moved me closer to something meaningful. Looking back, those difficult moments strengthened the resilience I carry today.

My educational journey was far from direct. There were times when I had to pause my studies because of health issues or financial strain. Each pause felt both frustrating and unfair, testing my determination more than I expected. The interruptions were discouraging, especially when earning my degree already felt like a long road. I often questioned whether I was strong enough to continue or if I would ever reach the goals I had set for myself. The uncertainty weighed on me, but I learned how to move through those moments of doubt. I reached out to mentors who encouraged me to view these pauses as moments for growth rather than failures. I used the time to reassess my goals and the steps I needed to take to reach them. I looked for resources, attended workshops on stress management, and connected with people who understood the challenges I faced. Through all of this, I learned the value of resilience and the impact of keeping a clear mindset.

During these breaks, I engaged in activities that strengthened my resolve and added meaning to my life. I volunteered in community programs, which helped others and gave me a stronger sense of purpose. These experiences reminded me that education was both a privilege and a tool for change. I remember working at a local food bank, helping distribute meals to families in need. The gratitude I saw in their eyes made me appreciate the moments I had previously taken for granted. Interacting with people from different backgrounds gave me a deeper understanding of the realities many face every day. I also looked-for part-time work that, while not always connected to my field of study, taught me practical skills and kept me grounded. I learned how to communicate clearly, work as part of a team, and adapt to changing situations. These skills later became important in my career. Working in unfamiliar roles pushed me out of my comfort zone and helped me grow both personally and professionally. Whether I was taking orders at a fast-food counter or tutoring younger students, I took each job as a chance to learn. Over time, I became more confident in my abilities and began to trust my judgment.

Each return to school came with renewed focus and determination. Going back to college after a break was difficult, as I had to rebuild my academic routine and catch up on what I had missed. I often felt the weight of previous challenges, but I also understood that every setback had given me new insight and strength. I approached my studies with a clearer mindset, ready to understand material that once felt out of reach. I developed study techniques that matched my learning style, used mindfulness practices to manage stress, and found value in studying with classmates. I also started using digital tools to stay organized and monitor my progress. Time management became essential, and I built a schedule that allowed me to balance school, work, and self-care. I learned to value the connections I made, realizing my journey wasn't something I had to carry alone. I started forming study groups with peers who shared similar goals, and together we worked through the demands of our coursework. Those sessions often became support circles where we pushed each other forward through shared experiences. We celebrated each other's wins, no matter the size, and we stayed present for each other during setbacks.

In 2011, I accomplished something that once felt out of reach: I graduated from college. The ceremony meant more than walking across a stage. It marked resilience and earned progress. The day felt unreal, filled with emotions I couldn't fully describe. I remember stepping forward as the cheers of my family and friends rose around me and a steady pride built in my chest. During that moment, I felt the weight of the years that had brought me there. The late nights, the work, and the belief that refused to break. Holding my diploma, I understood it represented more than academic success. It reflected a path of healing, growth, and strength that refused to collapse. My eyes filled with tears as I thought about the people who supported me along the way—my mentors, classmates, and family.

I felt a deep sense of gratitude for every lesson, obstacle, and breakthrough. Graduation didn't just mark the end of my academic journey. It validated the sacrifices I made to reach that point. It was a moment of personal vindication, proving that even after facing my deepest fears, I could still move toward what I wanted. The diploma in my hand felt heavy with the weight of my past yet light with the promise of my future. I knew with certainty that if I could overcome what I had survived, I could handle anything ahead of me. This accomplishment strengthened my belief in my own resilience, a belief I had earned through hard battles. Walking off that stage, I carried not just a degree but a renewed sense of direction and a steady confidence in what waited for me next.

Graduation marked the end of one path and the beginning of another. The excitement was real, and so was the uncertainty. Entering the workforce became the next challenge. The job market was competitive, and I had to prove my value beyond academic records. I learned quickly that while my degree mattered, my experiences shaped my advantage. My resume held a range of meaningful experiences that showed my ability to adapt and move through adversity. I took the time to shape a clear message around my journey, highlighting not only my academic progress but the skills and discipline I built through everything I faced.

I learned to communicate my story with clarity, using my experiences to connect with potential employers. I practiced telling it with honesty and direction, showing how adversity shaped my character. Finding a job that aligned with my qualifications and goals took time. I faced rejections and setbacks, but each one became a lesson.

I revised my resume many times, asked mentors for feedback, and practiced interview techniques with consistency. I attended workshops, joined career support groups, and treated networking as a core habit. The process was exhausting at times, but I refused to stop. Each rejection, even when it hurt, gave me another chance to grow, adjust my approach, and build confidence. Every "no" moved me closer to the right "yes." I treated each interview as an opportunity to show my skills and share the lessons I earned through experience. The setbacks taught me patience and strengthened my resolve. I became skilled at turning perceived weaknesses into strengths, showing how my experiences made me a more capable and empathetic candidate. This period of job searching pushed me to understand my own value and clarify what I wanted in a career. I learned that the right opportunity was not only about qualifications but also about alignment with my purpose and the person I had become.

In time, I secured a position that used my skills and matched my desire to help others. I began working at a nonprofit organization focused on supporting individuals with disabilities. This job was more than employment; it reflected my journey and gave me a platform to create meaningful change. My experiences had built empathy and resilience, qualities that shaped the way I approached the work. Each day gave me a chance to make a difference in someone's life, and I approached every interaction with intention. I worked closely with individuals who faced challenges similar to mine and offered support and encouragement grounded in my own path. It felt like a full circle moment, turning past pain into present purpose. I listened, advocated, and stood beside people who needed a voice.

Each day reminded me that strength can exist inside vulnerability and that shared experiences can move others toward healing. My role allowed me to push for change and help ensure that individuals with disabilities received the support and resources they deserved. I worked with educators, families, and policymakers to build programs that included everyone. Through this work, I learned what service really means: lifting others while continuing to grow myself.

As I moved through this experience, I realized that success rarely follows a straight path. It usually involves uncertainty and obstacles, yet these challenges reveal a person's true strength. My journey from finishing high school to finding my place in the workforce showed me how far determination and steady support can take someone. I still carry the lessons from my education, knowing that every challenge made me stronger. I meet each day with gratitude and confidence, ready for whatever comes next, encouraged by the fact that I can get through difficult moments and rise from them.

Life still brings new challenges, but I now see them as chances to grow. I've learned to face uncertainty with more calm, and I view failure as information, not a personal defeat. My story is not only about struggle. It is about resilience, hope, and the strength that can grow when education and community work together. As I look toward the future, I feel energized by the opportunities still ahead, knowing my journey is far from finished. I move forward with both ambition and a mission to give back, uplift others, and encourage people who face challenges similar to mine.

I held on to the idea of perseverance and reminded myself that every small win counted on the road to recovery. During difficult moments, it was easy to lose sight of progress. The challenges in front of me felt heavy, and they often covered up the quiet steps I was already taking. But I came to understand that each bit of progress, no matter how small, was a real achievement. Standing without help, speaking a full sentence clearly, or writing my name without hesitation were all moments worth recognizing.

These simple actions marked major breakthroughs in my healing. They showed me that progress does not need to be dramatic. It can be quiet, personal, and still deeply meaningful. By paying attention to these moments, I shifted my perspective. Instead of focusing only on what I had not yet reached, I began to notice the ground I had already covered.

Each small win strengthened my confidence and reminded me of what I was capable of. These moments encouraged me to keep moving, even when the path felt long. This shift in mindset changed how I approached challenges. Instead of viewing them as heavy barriers, I saw them as steps I could eventually climb. I learned to celebrate my effort just as much as the results.

Philippians 4:13 says, "I can do all things through Him who strengthens me." This verse became my lifeline and reminded me that I was not walking this path alone. In moments of doubt, when the weight of my struggles felt heavy, I turned to these words for comfort and strength. They showed me that my strength did not come from my own effort alone, but from a greater source. Through faith, I found the courage to face each challenge, knowing I was supported by something beyond my own ability. I felt guided, lifted when I was too weak to stand, and encouraged to keep moving even when the path was unclear. This belief helped me push through the darkest moments and rise above fear, giving me the resolve to continue with hope.

Faith became my anchor and kept me steady when everything else felt uncertain. It gave me a sense of peace that allowed me to keep going even when nothing around me made sense. It reminded me that nothing was impossible with faith. No challenge was too large or too overwhelming as long as I held on to my belief in God and trusted in the power of perseverance. Each time I recited that verse, I felt a renewed sense of direction. I learned to trust not only the process but also the presence of divine guidance along the way.

CHAPTER 7

Professional Life

"Education is not preparation for life; education is life itself."
– John Dewey.

Transitioning from student to educator was a meaningful and rewarding shift in my life. It was more than a career choice. It marked a personal evolution that allowed me to bring my experiences full circle. Working in school systems gave me the chance to give back to the community that had supported me throughout my journey. For the first time, I was not only receiving knowledge but shaping it, sharing it, and helping others grow.

The move from learning to teaching felt natural, almost like stepping into a role I had been preparing for all along. I was ready to apply everything I had learned, academically and through my own challenges, to guide the next generation. It gave me the opportunity to help create the kind of supportive and motivating environment I had benefited from, but now from the other side of the desk.

Early on, I worked in several roles, from administrative positions to classroom assistantships. Each one gave me insight into how schools operate beyond the lessons taught. These roles helped me understand the layers of policy, communication, and teamwork required to support a single student's success. That understanding made me more compassionate—not only toward students, but also toward educators and families.

My experiences as a student with special needs shaped my approach to teaching and administration. I carried the memory of feeling unseen and made a personal commitment to ensure no child would feel that way on my watch. I understood the challenges students with disabilities and learning difficulties face, and that awareness drove me to advocate for more inclusive educational practices. I collaborated closely with special education departments to design and implement programs that addressed diverse learning needs.

I did not want to simply meet educational standards; I wanted to meet students where they were. This often required creative approaches—adapting lesson plans, reevaluating communication strategies, and advocating for accommodations that were sometimes overlooked or misunderstood. Over time, I developed a toolkit that combined empathy with practicality, ensuring that every student felt supported.

Some days were harder than others. I often sat across from students who reminded me of my younger self—nervous, struggling, yet full of potential. I could see the fear in their eyes when a lesson didn't make sense or the frustration when their efforts went unnoticed. These moments reminded me why I chose this path. It was a privilege to offer the understanding and support I once needed. I aimed to be the steady hand that guided them, the patient voice reassuring them they were not alone. Seeing their small breakthroughs—the lightbulb moment when a concept clicked or the proud smile after overcoming a challenge—was deeply rewarding. Their successes became mine, and their struggles fueled my determination. Knowing I could make even a small difference in their journey made every difficult day worthwhile.

I structured my paraprofessional classroom intentionally. I did not want students to feel like just another name on a roster. I wanted them to know they mattered and that their voices carried weight. I built check-ins into our daily routine—short conversations where I asked how they were doing, not just academically but emotionally. Sometimes those brief exchanges revealed more than any test score ever could.

Building relationships with students and their families was one of the most fulfilling parts of my job. I saw reflections of my own struggles and triumphs in the students I mentored. Every child had a story, just like I did. Their progress, no matter how small, demonstrated the power of education and the importance of supportive environments. Through my work, I aimed to create spaces where every student felt valued and capable of reaching their potential.

I reminded myself that behind every challenging behavior was a need—unmet, unspoken, or misunderstood. My job was not just to teach content; it was to identify those needs and respond with compassion. Sometimes, all it took was a patient ear, a word of encouragement, or a small adjustment in how a lesson was delivered.

Connecting with families added another layer of depth to my work. I wanted them to feel like partners in their child's education, not outsiders looking in. I made it a priority to reach out regularly, not just when problems arose. I celebrated milestones with them, both big and small. A student's first full sentence written without assistance or a week of sustained focus in class became a shared victory.

These relationships became bridges between the classroom and home. Parents began to trust me with their worries, hopes, and feedback. I listened, learned, and adapted. Sometimes those conversations opened doors to solutions that changed how a student engaged in learning. Other times, they simply offered reassurance that someone truly cared.

I found that the more I understood a child's background, the better equipped I was to teach them. Socioeconomic struggles, cultural differences, or emotional trauma were not abstract concepts—they appeared in homework left incomplete, tempers lost, or eyes that avoided contact. Instead of judgment, I offered understanding. Instead of punishment, I offered support. This approach helped me look beyond surface behaviors and recognize the underlying challenges a student might face. It transformed my role from delivering content to becoming a true advocate for their wellbeing. I learned that a nurturing environment could unlock potential that traditional methods often overlooked. Building trust was essential, and it began with validating their experiences. When students felt seen and heard, their willingness to engage and learn grew significantly.

In my paraprofessional classroom, I created space for students to be themselves. Whether that meant a quiet corner for moments of overwhelm or allowing them to express ideas in nontraditional ways—through art, storytelling, or music—I encouraged authenticity. When students felt safe to show up as they were, their confidence grew.

Over time, I witnessed breakthroughs that were remarkable. Students who had once been withdrawn became leaders in group projects. Those who once dreaded coming to school began participating with joy. These changes did not happen overnight; they were built day by day through consistency, patience, and genuine care.

Each of these moments reaffirmed my belief in the importance of inclusive education—not just as a strategy, but as a philosophy. It is about seeing every student as capable, every challenge as an opportunity, and every success as a shared achievement.

The work was not easy, but it was meaningful. Every time a student's eyes lit up with understanding, or a parent said, "Thank you for seeing my child," I knew I was exactly where I was meant to be. A simple smile from a student or a grateful word from a parent reinforced why I chose this path. These moments stayed with me, quiet affirmations that I was in the right place. They fueled me on tougher days, a reminder of the impact I could have. It was more than a job; it was a calling that resonated with my own journey. Seeing students thrive because they felt understood and supported was the greatest reward.

While working in the school system, I felt a growing desire to further my education. Pursuing advanced studies became increasingly appealing. It was not just about career advancement; it was about deepening my understanding of educational theories and practices and equipping myself with tools to make a more significant impact.

I wanted to make informed decisions rooted in research, not just instinct. I craved a deeper understanding of how systems work and how they could be improved. My goal was not just to be a better teacher—it was to be a stronger advocate, a more effective leader, and a lifelong learner.

Balancing work with academic studies was a formidable challenge. The demands of my job were considerable, and adding a rigorous academic schedule required careful time management and unwavering dedication. At times, exhaustion threatened to derail my efforts, but the drive to improve myself—and, by extension, the educational experiences of my students—kept me going.

The program opened new vistas of knowledge. Courses in educational leadership, curriculum development, and inclusive practices were especially impactful. They gave me more than academic insight—they reshaped how I viewed my role in education. These courses provided both theoretical foundations and practical tools to make meaningful changes in the school system. I began revisiting classroom practices with a fresh perspective and approached administrative decisions with greater intentionality.

My academic pursuits also rekindled a long-dormant passion for learning. I remembered what it felt like to be intellectually challenged, to read with curiosity, and to write with purpose. The program didn't just equip me professionally; it reminded me that education is a lifelong journey. As I grew in knowledge, I also grew in empathy for students navigating their own academic paths and for colleagues striving to improve their craft.

Pursuing my studies while working full time was an intense juggling act. The demands were constant, and the margin for error was small. Balancing professional responsibilities, academic commitments, and personal life required structure, discipline, and resilience. Some days felt impossibly long. Mornings began before sunrise with quiet study sessions, and nights often ended at the dining table surrounded by open textbooks and unfinished lesson plans.

Time management became more than a skill; it became a survival strategy. I learned to break large goals into smaller, manageable tasks. I scheduled everything, including rest and meals. Weekends became sacred blocks of study time, while weekdays demanded complete focus on teaching and school leadership. There was little room for spontaneity, but I accepted this season as one of growth, not comfort.

At times, I questioned whether I had taken on too much. Doubt crept in during late nights or after difficult workdays, when exhaustion blurred my sense of purpose. But I always returned to my "why"—the students I served, the educators I supported, and the long-term change I envisioned. I knew the sacrifices were temporary, but the impact could be lasting.

I leaned heavily on my support system. Mentors offered guidance when I felt stuck, helping me see problems from different angles. Peers in the program became allies, sharing resources, listening without judgment, and celebrating even the smallest milestones. And my family? They were my anchor. Their patience, encouragement, and unwavering belief in me gave me strength during the lowest points.

Personal life didn't pause just because my schedule was full. Relationships with family and friends were lifelines I had to protect, even when time was limited. I made conscious efforts to stay connected through quick calls, shared meals, or simple check-ins. These connections grounded me. They reminded me that while professional goals mattered, so did joy, rest, and emotional wellbeing.

There were trade-offs, of course. I missed gatherings. I said no to vacations. My social life thinned, and self-care sometimes took a backseat. But I also learned the importance of boundaries. I began to recognize signs of burnout and made space for recovery when needed—whether through a walk outside, a few pages of a novel, or a quiet hour without a screen.

Looking back, the journey through my studies wasn't just about earning a degree. It was about growth—intellectual, emotional, and professional. It stretched me beyond what I thought I could manage. It taught me that commitment and vision could coexist with fatigue and vulnerability. Most importantly, it reaffirmed my belief that with the right tools, support, and mindset, it is possible to do hard things—and do them well.

As I reflect on this chapter of my life, the impact of education stands out as a defining influence. My professional journey, shaped by roles within school systems and the pursuit of knowledge, has been closely intertwined with my personal growth. I became more patient, more introspective, and more confident in my ability to lead and inspire.

Education has been the cornerstone of my resilience and adaptability. It has provided me with the skills and knowledge to navigate challenges and overcome obstacles. More importantly, it has instilled in me a sense of purpose and a drive to make a meaningful difference in the lives of others.

The journey from student, through personal adversity, to educator has been transformative. Each step reinforced my belief that education is a powerful tool for change—one capable of elevating individuals and creating ripple effects that extend across entire communities.

One of the most important lessons I learned during my transition into education was the value of inclusivity. In the classroom, diversity extends beyond ethnicity or culture; it includes different learning styles, abilities, and life experiences. As a student with special needs, I was often placed in environments that did not accommodate my learning style, making the educational experience both frustrating and isolating. As an educator, I was determined to create a different experience for my students.

I vividly recall my first assignment as a paraprofessional. I was tasked with developing a lesson plan for a group of fourth graders. My goal was to teach the water cycle using multiple learning modalities. I incorporated visual aids, hands-on experiments, and collaborative group work to ensure that every child could engage with the material. During the lesson, I watched students who typically struggled with traditional methods begin to shine. Their excitement was evident, reaffirming my belief in the necessity of inclusive education.

Moments like that stayed with me. They reminded me that when students feel seen and supported, their potential expands.

Incorporating technology was another way to enhance inclusivity. Many students thrive when given the chance to use digital resources. I began integrating educational apps and online platforms that catered to different learning styles. For example, auditory learners benefited from podcasts, while visual learners engaged with interactive videos. Technology not only made learning more engaging but also gave students greater autonomy over their learning.

Inclusivity, however, is not just about adapting teaching methods—it must be embedded in a school's culture. I focused on creating an environment where every student felt safe, seen, and respected. This meant addressing bullying, prejudice, and isolation directly. I led workshops on empathy, cultural understanding, and emotional intelligence, encouraging students to view one another with compassion rather than judgment. Celebrating diversity became part of our daily practice, not just a theme for one month each year.

Working with families was equally critical. I believed that when schools and homes collaborated, students thrived. I kept open lines of communication with parents through newsletters, conferences, and community events. These interactions helped me understand each child's background and tailor support accordingly. I also hosted workshops to guide parents in supporting learning at home, particularly for students facing academic or emotional challenges.

One student, Mia, stands out in my memory. She struggled with reading and often withdrew during class activities. In a conference, her mother shared that Mia felt anxious about falling behind her peers. This insight prompted me to design a personalized reading plan with books aligned to Mia's interests and experiences. Gradually, Mia regained her confidence. Her joy in reading returned, and her academic growth followed. Witnessing her transformation reinforced the importance of treating every student as an individual with unique needs and strengths.

These experiences strengthened my belief that learning extends far beyond the classroom. It happens in relationships, in homes, and in the quiet moments when a student feels seen and heard. This philosophy also guided my professional development. I consistently sought opportunities to grow—through workshops, webinars, and conversations with fellow educators.

One of the most impactful experiences was training on trauma-informed teaching. I began to see classroom disruptions not as defiance but as signals of deeper emotional struggles. This perspective shifted my approach. I introduced mindfulness practices, including morning breathing exercises and reflection time. The results were clear: students became more focused, calm, and engaged.

I also participated in a mentorship program that paired experienced educators with newer teachers. The relationships I built were invaluable. We exchanged ideas, shared challenges, and supported each other in navigating the complexities of the profession. These collaborations became a consistent source of renewal and inspiration.

Over time, I grew into a mentor, leading professional development sessions on inclusive practices and behavior management. Sharing what I had learned was deeply fulfilling and reinforced my own understanding. I also immersed myself in educational literature. One book that profoundly shaped my thinking was Mindset by Carol Dweck. Her insights into the power of a growth mindset aligned perfectly with my belief in students' capacity to evolve and overcome obstacles.

This mindset became central to my teaching. I encouraged students to embrace challenges and learn from mistakes, modeling that behavior myself. I shared my own learning journey with them—how I balanced work, studies, and personal responsibilities—and demonstrated that struggle and success often go hand in hand.

One former student, Kevin, stands out. He battled severe anxiety and initially found it difficult to participate in class. Over time, with personalized strategies and consistent encouragement, he began to open up. Years later, I received a letter from him saying he had become a counselor to help others like himself. It was a full-circle moment—one that reaffirmed my commitment to this work.

As I advanced in my career, I realized that individual efforts were not enough. Systemic change was necessary. I began participating in policy discussions and advocacy groups focused on equitable education. I advocated for increased funding for special education, mental health resources, and professional training on inclusion.

These collective efforts are part of a larger mission. Being an educator is not just about delivering content—it is about fostering an environment where every student can thrive. Looking ahead, I am excited about the opportunities before me. The field of education is evolving, and I am committed to being an active participant in that journey. Each day presents a new chance to make a difference, inspire students, and cultivate an environment where every individual feels valued and capable. Education is not just a profession for me; it is a lifelong mission to empower others and create positive change in the world.

In this journey, I am reminded that every student has a story, and each story deserves respect, understanding, and support. This belief drives me to continue advocating for an inclusive and equitable education system—one where every student can reach their fullest potential. I look forward to the next chapter of my journey, confident that my experiences and dedication to education will continue to shape not only my life but also the lives of those I serve.

I carry with me the stories of my students—their struggles, triumphs, and growth. Each story reminds me of the transformative power of education. As I look ahead, I remain deeply committed to this path. The work is never finished, and that is its beauty. There is always more to learn, more to give, and more lives to touch.

CHAPTER 8

Parallel Experiences - Good and Bad

"Although the world is full of suffering, it is also full of the overcoming of it." – **Helen Keller**

Life is filled with both joy and sorrow. As I reflect on my journey, I see a pattern of parallel experiences—moments of triumph alongside periods of struggle. These dualities have shaped me, teaching critical lessons about resilience and the human spirit.

The positive experiences often came as unexpected blessings amid hardships. After surviving the traumatic events of 1990, each small victory—relearning to walk, completing high school, or earning my degree—felt monumental. These achievements mattered not only for their immediate significance, but for what they represented: perseverance and the network of support that surrounded me.

Yet persistent challenges remained. The physical and emotional scars from the gunshot wounds were constant reminders of my ordeal. There were days of excruciating pain, moments of self-doubt, and periods of profound frustration. Navigating these difficulties demanded an inner strength that was tested repeatedly. Accepting life's complexities meant recognizing that joy and struggle are not mutually exclusive; they coexist, continuously shaping one another. The exhilaration of triumph felt sweeter because of the hardships endured, and the struggles revealed lessons that fueled my personal growth.

This understanding allowed me to embrace life's full spectrum, appreciating both highs and lows. Healing was rarely linear—it was complex and often unpredictable. Moments of doubt and hope intertwined throughout my recovery, creating a layered and meaningful experience. There were days when the weight of my past felt unbearable, yet those same days often contained the seeds of endurance that would later flourish.

It was in these moments of struggle that I learned the meaning of perseverance, discovering strength I didn't know I possessed. The journey taught me that setbacks were not failures but detours on the path to growth. I began to see my past not as a burden, but as a foundation for building a stronger future.

The scars, both visible and hidden, became part of my identity, shaping not only who I was but who I aspired to become.

Therapy played an essential role in this journey. Speaking with a counselor provided a safe space to untangle complex feelings and fears. Each session revealed insights long obscured by pain. Through this process, I learned to give voice to my emotions, recognizing vulnerability not as weakness but as an act of courage—a gateway to healing. My therapist's office became a sanctuary where I could unpack the heavy burdens I had been carrying. It was a space where I felt truly seen and understood, without judgment.

Slowly, with guidance, I began to reframe my narrative, shifting from victim to survivor. I learned to treat myself with the same compassion I would offer a friend. This newfound self-acceptance became a powerful catalyst, propelling me further along the path to recovery.

Alongside therapy, writing became a personal refuge. Penning my thoughts and experiences offered a cathartic release, helping me map my journey and reflect on its lessons. Writing directed my pain into purpose. Through storytelling, I found a way to connect with others facing their own battles. Sharing my story was not only healing but an invitation for others to find hope and strength in theirs. Every word I wrote felt like a step away from the shadows and closer to the light. It allowed me to reclaim my narrative and turn the chaos of my past into something coherent and meaningful.

The blank page became a silent, nonjudgmental confidante, holding space for every raw emotion. Through writing, I discovered a voice I did not know I had, capable of expressing both profound sorrow and resilience. This outlet became a powerful tool for self-discovery and a bridge to deeper understanding of myself.

Through this process, I came to appreciate the value of community. In my darkest moments, the unwavering support of friends and family became a lifeline. Their faith in me sparked a fire that fueled my determination to endure. I realized our stories are often interconnected, and it is within these shared experiences that we find comfort and solidarity.

Volunteering in my community soon became an essential part of my healing. I sought to mirror the support I had received by giving back to others facing their own challenges. Engaging empathically with those in need nurtured my spirit and reinforced our shared humanity. In these interactions, I witnessed firsthand how each individual journey contributes to the broader richness of life.

Embracing gratitude gave new purpose to my days. It became a conscious practice to acknowledge and appreciate beauty in both joy and sorrow. I kept a gratitude journal, noting three things each day that brought me joy, no matter how small. This habit not only helped me focus on the positive but also trained my mind to seek out good in every situation. I began noticing the vibrant colors of flowers in bloom, the kindness of strangers, and the warmth of a hug.

This perspective allowed me to move through life with a lighter heart and an openness to renewal each morning. I realized that gratitude is not merely a fleeting feeling but a lens through which to view the world. It influenced my interactions, deepening connections with others and fostering a sense of community. I found joy in giving back, whether through volunteering or offering a listening ear to a friend in need.

As I embraced gratitude, I discovered that it also strengthened my adaptability. When challenges appeared, I learned to meet them with appreciation, recognizing that difficulties could still teach meaningful lessons. This shift in thinking helped me face adversity with greater courage, knowing that each struggle carried its own opportunity for growth.

Over time, gratitude became a guiding principle. It showed me that even in the darkest moments, there is always something to be thankful for, whether it is a lesson learned, a connection made, or a brief moment of beauty that reminds us of the good still present in the world. By choosing gratitude, I renewed my own life and encouraged those around me to look for their own moments of appreciation, creating a quiet ripple of positivity and hope.

As time passed, I learned to see vulnerability as a form of strength. Society often associates it with weakness, yet I discovered that it opens the door to connection and growth. Sharing my struggles required real courage, and doing so encouraged others to share their own. Through that openness, we formed deeper bonds and built communities shaped by understanding.

This sensitivity extended beyond my personal story. It pushed me to advocate for people who felt unheard and to take part in conversations about mental health, trauma, and strength. I wanted to challenge stigma and create spaces where people could speak honestly and find support. In advocating for others, I found renewed purpose, turning my own pain into shared awareness and connection.

Looking back, I see that second chances are more than opportunities for personal growth. They become legacies we pass forward. Each time I offered compassion or understanding, I contributed to a cycle of hope. In these moments—quiet but meaningful—we help build a more empathetic and supportive society.

My life story is shaped by many second chances—not only my own, but also those I have been fortunate to witness in others. I often think about the students I worked with, many carrying heavy challenges. When I shared my journey, I saw something shift in them. They realized that setbacks do not define who we are; they reveal what we can still become. Together, we explored the strength that comes from recognizing the new opportunities life offers.

Most importantly, I learned to extend grace to myself. As I worked toward my goals, I came to understand that failure is not a dead end but a stage in the process. Just as I offered patience and understanding to others, I began offering the same inward. Each misstep became part of my growth, reminding me that a meaningful life is shaped by experience, not by flawlessly avoiding mistakes.

As I close this chapter, I invite you to reflect on your own story—its turning points, challenges, and quiet victories. What patterns have shaped your life, and how have they influenced who you are today? Each of us carries a story built from joy and hardship, and those experiences connect us to others in ways we often overlook. The path we walk is never isolated; it reflects both our individual journey and the shared movement of the people we encounter along the way.

Take a moment to think about the second chances you have received and the ones you have offered to others. These moments of grace can become turning points that help you grow in ways you didn't expect. Embrace the experiences that shaped you, welcoming both triumph and struggle as necessary parts of your journey. Every challenge faced and every victory earned adds meaning to your life, forming a story that belongs only to you.

Life is a continuing cycle of learning and renewal, and it is through this cycle that you discover your strength. Each day gives you an opening to begin again, learn from the past, and move forward with hope and determination. I encourage you to greet each day with gratitude, recognizing the potential for new beginnings. Notice the beauty in the ordinary and the extraordinary, because both carry lessons that can enrich your life.

Let vulnerability work for you, allowing your story to unfold with honesty. Embracing it opens the door to deeper connections with others, building empathy and understanding. When we share our stories, we create bridges of inspiration and connection that ease the feeling of isolation.

By doing this, we form a community of shared experiences, where each voice adds depth to the larger human story.

As you move through your own journey, remember that it is okay to stumble and fall. Each misstep is an opening to grow, a moment to learn more about yourself and the world around you. Give yourself the grace to be imperfect, to accept the messiness of life, and to find strength in your struggles.

Every experience in your life matters. The bright moments of joy and the harder moments of sorrow both shape your growth. Together, they form a story that reflects who you are now and who you are becoming. As you reflect on your life, think about how you can bring in new moments of hope, perseverance, and connection that support the direction you want to go.

Let your story show the power of perseverance and the durability of the human spirit. Embrace the path ahead, knowing that each day gives you another chance to add meaning to your life and inspire those around you. When we recognize the patterns of our lives, we also see how connected we are to one another, each of us contributing to a larger human story.

Let us celebrate the depth of life and the many ways our experiences shape us. When we accept both light and shadow, we open ourselves to the full range of what it means to exist. Together, we create stories that reflect endurance, hope, and the power of second chances.

Throughout my journey, I've learned that our lives often connect in subtle and meaningful ways. Every person we meet—friends, mentors, even strangers—adds something to our growth. These connections remind us that we are not isolated. Our individual stories contribute to something larger than ourselves.

I have also learned the value of listening. Each person carries their own challenges, and by offering genuine attention, we create spaces where people feel safe enough to be themselves. Sometimes, presence alone becomes the gift that strengthens both others and ourselves.

Beyond personal healing, giving back has become a way to honor my own path. By supporting those in need, I channel my past struggles into meaningful action and remind myself that even in dark moments, each of us can still create something positive.

I now trust that every experience—joyful or painful—serves a purpose in shaping the person we become. I encourage you to value your own story and share it with confidence. When we do, we strengthen a sense of resilience, community, and hope. Even the difficult parts of your journey contribute to its meaning. Every scar reflects survival, strength, and the spirit to keep moving forward. Let your vulnerability work in your favor.

It connects you to others who are navigating their own challenges. Your path, in all its honesty, has the power to encourage and uplift. Move forward not only with hope, but with the steady awareness that your life, with its struggles and its victories, shows the depth of the human heart and its capacity to endure.

About the Author

Thomas Smith was born and raised in Detroit, Michigan. He is the son of the late Yvonne Smith and Thomas Barber. He grew up in a loving family with his brothers Darren, Anthony, and Donald, and his sister Danielle. His upbringing in Detroit shaped his character, faith, and determination.

Thomas is a devoted father and grandfather. He cherishes his daughters, sons, and grandchildren, and he honors the memory of his son De'Terrious Jerome Hayes, who has passed away. His extended family, including cousins, friends, and loved ones, continues to be a strong source of inspiration and purpose in his life.

Thomas's journey has been marked by resilience. After facing a life-threatening season when his family believed they might lose him, he reached a deep spiritual turning point. God's intervention restored his life, strengthened his faith, and renewed his commitment to living with purpose.

Guided by his family's long-held motto, "Pray together, stay together," Thomas lives by unity, love, and the power of prayer. These values continue to carry him through every challenge.

A Second Chance reflects his story of survival, faith, and the steady strength of family. Through his writing, Thomas hopes to encourage others to trust in God's grace and hold close the people who matter most.

www.ingramcontent.com/pod-product-compliance
Lightning Source LLC
Chambersburg PA
CBHW051224120626
46547CB00013B/1499

* 9 7 8 1 9 6 6 6 1 2 9 6 4 *